Gambling Collectibles

A Sure Winner

Leonard Schneir

Schiffer Publishing Ltd

77 Lower Valley Road, Atglen, PA 19310

JAMES CAGNEY in "FRISCO KID" - a Warner Bros First National Picture RE-RELEASE

Title page:
1935: Evan's Deluxe Horse Race Wheel This reverse painting on glass gaming wheel, which featured famous thoroughbreds, including Gallant Fox, is five feet in diameter and mounted on an eight foot post. The wheel offered odds ranging from five-to-one to fifteen-to-one. The claim in the catalog in which it was offered for sale was, "It never fails to get a play while netting the house a handsome percentage."

Above:
c. 1935: "Frisco Kid" Theatre Lobby Photo Here is a young Jimmy Cagney as a spectator to a pharo game, pointing to the dealer as he reaches for the coins on the pharo board. Although often pictured in rough saloons, pharo was also played in elegant casinos such as this one.

Right:
c. 1900-1910: Six Advertising Aces of Spades Various product ads were printed on decks of playing cards. The products advertised on these Aces were also featured on the backs, jokers, and boxes of the decks.

GAMBLING COLLECTIBLES : A Sure Winner

Copyright © 1993 by Leonard Schneir
Library of Congress Number: 93-085215

ISBN: 0-88740-541-X

Layout by Bonnie Hensley

Published by Schiffer Publishing Ltd.
77 Lower Valley Road
Atglen, Pennsylvania 19310
This book may be purchased from the publisher.
Please include $2.95 for postage.
Try your bookstore first

We are interested in hearing from authors
with book ideas on related subjects

DEDICATION

This book is dedicated to Merlin who always helps to make my dreams come true, and to my mother, for teaching me the difference between right and wrong.

ACKNOWLEDGEMENTS

I would like to express my gratitude to all of the collectors who have helped me with this book by providing photographs of items in their collections, as well as sharing useful information about gambling collectibles. Thanks to Al Cali, Judy and Tom Dawson, Pryor Dodge, Robert Eisenstadt, Bernie Gold, Frank Goldberg, Gene Hochman, Larry Lubliner, Sidney Radner, Dale Seymour, Russell Umbraco, Ron Wohl, Susan Jarvis (Director of the Gaming Resource Center at the University of Nevada Library, Las Vegas) and Dennis, her assistant, who assisted me. I also want to thank the friendly staff at The Gambler's Book Club in Las Vegas. And a very special thanks to "The Cincinnati Kid" Bob Rosenberger who helped and encouraged me all along the way.

My appreciation to editor Douglas Congdon-Martin and publisher Peter Schiffer for having faith and taking a chance.

Photography credits to: Douglas Congdon-Martin, Jeffrey Snyder, Steve Bowling, Al Cali, Steve Crowley, Tom Dawson, Andrea Hamilton, Russell Umbraco and Sidney Radner.

TABLE OF CONTENTS

The fascinating history of poker as it relates to pioneering America, including photographs of poker collectibles such as rare ivory bucks, the colorful graphics of unusual antique books and magazines on poker, turn of the century photos of people playing poker, Poker Alice, and a well known series of paintings of poker games as they were played across the country. Includes bibliography of books on poker from 1836-1941. As John Blackbridge said in 1875, poker is, "The American National Game."

A visual history of gambling as portrayed on numerous antique photographs and postcards with gambling themes and scenes. Includes nostalgic pictures of Early Western gambling halls, clubs and casinos, offshore gambling ships, cowboys and Indians gambling, turn of the century Monte Carlo, Interior scenes of Early Nevada and Juarez casinos and clubs with slot machines, and other gambling scenes.

Turn of the century advertising items each using images of gambling and playing cards to sell their products. Includes trade cards, cookie tins, tin lithographed trays advertising beer and whiskey, cigar boxes, cigar labels, tip trays, ash trays, tobacco tins, promotional posters, cigarettes, shaving items, decks of cards and clay poker chips.

Publicity photos and theater lobby cards of dramatic gambling scenes in Hollywood films from the thirties to the sixties. Includes Ronald Reagan, Nancy Reagan, Jimmy Cagney, Abbott and Costello, Clark Gable, Spencer Tracy, Jane Russell, Frank Sinatra, Elvis Presley, and many notable Western stars in movie gambling images.

An in-depth explanation of cheating and antique cheating devices, along with photographs of pages from the original catalogs that sold these items. Photos of marked and "prepared" cards, loaded dice, "hold-out" devices which were strapped on to the body to produce an ace or other card "as needed". Colorful covers and illustrations from early magazines and books. Much of this writing warns against con games and cheating systems, and the pitfalls of playing with cheaters.

The story of pharo, the most popular gambling game in America from about 1720 to 1870, starting in New Orleans and making its way to the mining towns of the West. Includes photos of regular and gaffed dealing boxes, rosewood casekeepers with ivory markers, hand painted layout boards, pharo cards and other pharo gaming equipment, as well as historic photos and movie scenes of people playing pharo. An explanation of how the great old game was played.

Antique ivory chips, circa 1840-1890, beautifully and elaborately hand-scrimshawed. Unique and flamboyant designs of flowers, animals, horseshoes, and other motifs, along with beautifully scripted numerals. Perhaps the fastest growing of all gambling collectibles, some ivory chips are as valuable as one thousand dollars for a single chip. This chapter also includes unusual gaming boxes which were made for chips used in poker and pharo.

High fashion gamblers of the past had very fancy pocket watches, some with enamelled playing cards on the dial, or miniature roulette wheels that actually worked. These were often sold through catalogs and were intended for play at home or at the local tavern. Includes photographs of these very beautifully crafted watches.

Anything goes in Wild Cards! A Diana Board, matchsafes and cigarette cases of silver and enamel, Monte Carlo souvenir spoons, antique card presses with bead work and ivory finials, unusual dice, prints, paintings, baseball playing cards, songsheets, lottery tickets and a horse racing carnival wheel. Also books and magazines related to gambling, even early comic books which featured gambling or playing card scenes on their covers. And a large walrus tusk from the Bella Union Saloon in San Francisco that was scrimshawed with card and gambling imagery in about 1855.

A history of playing cards and photographs of many of America's rarest decks, dating back to 1820. Several decks from the Civil War, the Seminole War Deck, a hand painted Confederate deck, cards with Buffalo Bill, Sitting Bull and Pocahontas, a Tiffany Transformation Deck, and unusual advertising, political, theater and sports related decks, as well as many other fascinating playing cards. Diverse paper ephemera from playing card companies. Includes a suggested reading list.

FOREWORD

Gambling, simply stated, is as American as baseball, hot dogs, and apple pie. Despite the best efforts of our Puritan forebearers, throughout its history America has been a country of rebels and gamblers. We've rebelled against the British, the French, the Indians...why, we even rebelled against ourselves during the Civil War. This rebellious spirit, when coupled with the inherent risk of leaving everything you've known and moving to a new land, has provided a fertile field for gambling.

In the 19th century, America's most popular gambling games were faro and poker. Faro evolved in Europe and arrived in this country, largely intact. Poker, on the other hand, is a distinctly American game. Where and when it originated, as well as the manner in which it evolved, are subject to debate and will be discussed in this book. Whatever its antecedents, however, poker has reflected the American spirit by catering to the bold, the bluffer, and the brazen. Both faro and poker have created a wealth of gambling collectibles. To collectors, they are among the most prized and most attractive. Other games, such as keno, hazard, roulette, etc., have produced similarly attractive items.

The intent of this book is to inform and amuse both the novice and the established collector of gambling paraphernalia. More subtly, it is my hope that it will "seduce" the non-collector into becoming one. On the pages of this book, you will see a myriad of gambling items, some exceedingly rare, others not nearly so. What makes them so inviting is that they are all attractive, and they have a certain aura of romance associated with them.

Take time to peruse this book. Unlike many other books on collectibles, this one contains a substantial amount of text. Once you've read some of it, and taken the time to gaze at the lovely pictures I think you will become as "hooked" as I have been for so many years.

The author and compiler of this book, Lenny Schneir, is an avid collector of gambling items - and a person with a special love for the turn of a playing card. Because so much misinformation exists in the area of gambling and gambling collectibles, Lenny has gone to great length to seek the truth and make it available to you in this book.

Bob Rosenberger
Jan. 8, 1993, Cincinnati

1910: "POKER GAME" Postcard Embossed postcard by S.A. Solomon. This card was an invitation to a poker game, the date and time to be filled in by the sender, who could also draw in the starting time by adding hands to the clock.

Introduction:
FOR OPENERS

We are a nation of gamblers. Our entire economy is built upon taking chances. Every business or financial judgment involves the possibilities of profit or loss. Starting any new business is a risk and a bank that lends capital to a new business is taking a risk. Speculating in the stock market which fluctuates up and down from day to day is taking a risk. Much like a good poker player, insurance companies try to carefully work out the odds and percentages when they sell life, health or property insurance but the element of risk is always there. Taking chances on futures and options in the commodity markets is not all that different from betting on your favorite football team or making a friendly wager.

The successful entrepreneur is the one who has made a long series of educated bets in which he or she has often been the winner. These bets might have been on how much merchandise to manufacture, or how much merchandise to purchase for inventory, which sources to purchase from, choosing a location, and even selecting employees from among all those who apply. Political candidates who spend huge sums of money on a campaign may not be gambling for personal economic gain but they are betting time, money and energy on the chance of winning a particular level of prestige and power.

c. 1900: Monte Carlo Roulette Postcard Embossed, with gold ink printing. Published by Artist Ateliers H. Guggenheim of Zurich. The glamorous woman is blowing bubbles with different roulette numbers. Her current bubble, a zero, is known as the "house number."

c. 1900: Monte Carlo Roulette Postcard The croupier wears the roulette wheel on her head, and a blindfold over her eyes, implying that it's all random luck as she lets the chips fall where they may.

Every personal decision we make involves taking risks of some kind. We are each gambling with our future when we decide whether or not to go to college and if the answer is yes, deciding upon which college to attend. We are gambling with our time and money when we decide upon a career and spend years training for it with the hope that we will continue to like that particular profession or job a decade or two later. We are gambling with our happiness when we decide whether or not to marry, and, if yes, whom to marry, and whether or not to have children, and, if yes, when. Even doing something as simple as crossing a busy street, or trying an unfamiliar restaurant, we are taking chances. We all gamble every day and in every way. Every decision in life is a gamble, some with much higher stakes than others.

Gambling is based upon risk taking and taking risks underlies the very nature of capitalism and entrepreneurial enterprise. The youth of any country might be well-served to grow up with a thorough understanding of winning and losing, following rules, odds, percentages, vigorish, edges, mathematics, numbers, strategy, competition and good sportsmanship, which are each learned in gambling games. It might help them to better understand if or when to take chances all throughout their lives. There is much to be gained from a society that permits gambling, especially when compared to a society that attempts to suppress all forms of gambling.

Gambling games are older than written history and have been known in just about every culture. There is evidence that gambling games were a part of society in ancient Egypt, Sumer, India, Canaan, China, Persia, Ethiopia, Greece, Rome, Ancient Germany and Viking Norway. Most of the indigenous peoples of North and South America played many different games and gambled extensively long before the arrival of Europeans. The cliff dwellers of the Southwest bet on contests of skill and games of chance, at times associating their bets with ancient legends of wagers made by the deities they revered. This idea of the gods gambling can also be found in an ancient Egyptian legend in which the god, Thoth, gambled with the moon; his win allowed the Egyptian gods, Isis and Osiris, to be born. It seems that an interest in gambling is quite primal, possibly instinctual among the entire human species, yet there is a considerable amount of disagreement about whether or not this interest should be legally curtailed.

Prior to 1880, there was "open gambling" in the United States and its territories, with very few laws regulating the many diverse forms of gambling. In fact, it was most often the Marshall, the Sheriff and the local government who were the proprietors and protectors of gambling establishments, which were among the earliest commercial enterprises in the developing towns and cities of America.

Our first and third presidents were avid card players and enjoyed gaming for money. There are numerous references to playing card games and betting in the private journals of both George Washington and Thomas Jefferson. Among Washington's earliest entries, January 16th, 1768, was "At home all day at cards. It's snowing." His journals show that he kept careful accounts of his wins and losses in games played at places such as Fredericksburg, Williamsburg and Annapolis, with other entries explaining that over a period of four years he lost only six pounds, three shillings and three pence. However, during the time of battle for our independence, he issued this order from Morristown, New Jersey on May 8th, 1777, "The Commander in Chief in the most pointed and explicit terms forbids all officers and soldiers playing at cards." Perhaps this was based upon his personal knowledge of how distracted the soldiers might become if they were too involved in a game of cards.

While running for his re-election as president of the United States in 1828, John Quincy Adams was accused of keeping gaming tables in the White House. Andrew Jackson won that election with 56% of the popular vote and 68% of the electoral college votes, even though it was well known that he was a gambler and owner of race horses. Jackson was described as, "the most roaring, rollicking, game cocking, horse racing, card playing, mischievous fellow that ever lived". Old Hickory's daring attitudes about taking risks and living life to the full, but always with courage and honor, clearly had a great appeal to the American voters.

Led by New York State in 1881, anti-gambling legislation began to sweep the nation and "open gambling" was gradually shut down. Gambling became a "morality issue" often invoked in political campaigns for election to state, city or county positions. The last state to make gambling illegal was Nevada, this legislation taking effect on Oct.1st,1910. (It was legalized again in 1931.)

1952: "The Las Vegas Story" with Jane Russell, Victor Mature and Vincent Price Made by R.K.O. Radio Pictures, the film was presented by Howard Hughes, who made several films starring Jane Russell. This scene in a Las Vegas Casino depicts Black Jack tables, a Chuck-a-Luck dice cage, and "The Last Chance" written ominously on the mirror over the bar.

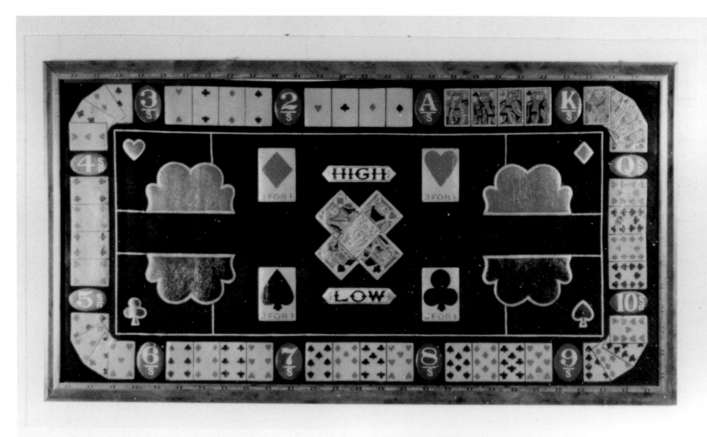

c. 1890: Diana Board Made by Wm. Suydam, located at 22 Union Square in New York City. Meticulously hand-painted on billiard cloth. The game of Diana had a betting format similar to roulette, using playing cards in place of the usual numbers. Diana never did become very popular because the odds offered to the player were extremely unfavorable, but the boards are some of the most beautiful items within the field of gambling collectibles and are greatly treasured. Courtesy of Sidney Radner.

"Why struggle in vain to eliminate gambling when the city can license, regulate and tax gambling activity." So said John W. Geary, Mayor of San Francisco in 1849. It appears that the thoughts of Mayor Geary have permeated the minds of many contemporary legislators. Increased interest in legalized gambling has often been a response to economic woes, when it is suddenly viewed as a viable source for raising public revenue.

Even as I write and prepare this book for publication, gambling in America has been going through a renaissance. Recent laws have made it possible to establish legal casinos with small limit stakes poker and slot machines in the old mining towns of South Dakota and Colorado. There is legal gambling in the poker parlors of California, on steamboats cruising along the Mississippi River, and in casinos on many Native American reservations across the country. Gambling was legalized in Atlantic City, New Jersey in 1978, leading to the construction of major casinos all along the boardwalk. The election of November, 1992 included referendums to legalize state-run lotteries in Georgia, Mississippi and Nebraska. Local referendums on gambling were on the ballot in Denver, Chicago and New Orleans.

All this has occurred alongside the previously established legal gambling of numerous state-run lotteries which began with New Hampshire in 1963. Added to this are the state run jai alai frontons, and betting on horse races both at the tracks and in off-track betting offices. Since gambling was legalized in Nevada in 1931, major gambling casinos and sports betting parlors have flourished in Lake Tahoe, Las Vegas and Reno, while smaller casinos, sports betting, and easy access to slot machines can be found all across the state.

How much revenue can the new forms of gambling raise? Some people have suggested a national lottery to cut the federal deficit.

Captain John Smith appreciated the British lotteries that helped the early seventeenth century Jamestown colony to survive. Benjamin Franklin, George Washington and John Hancock encouraged and participated in lotteries of the mid-eighteenth century to support public improvements. Contemporary city and state legislators faced with deficits, unbalanced budgets, overtaxed constituents and deteriorating public services are again turning toward legalizing various forms of gambling to help improve social services. Will government sponsored or approved gambling casinos, sports betting, slot machines, poker parlors, lotteries, horse race betting and other forms of gambling eventually be easily accessible to everyone in the country? Will gambling revenues become an important vehicle for solving our economic problems - or just another idea that doesn't work?

Whatever decisions are made about legalizing gambling, all games must be structured, played and regulated with the highest degree of integrity and honesty, or the idea will certainly fail. It is interesting to note that in ancient India, according to archaeologist A.L. Basham, there were, "officially managed gambling houses with a charge for the hire of dice to gamblers, who were forbidden to use their own. Stringent fines were laid down for cheating."

No matter what the legal decisions, gambling and especially card playing have long been and still are widespread activities in our culture. They permeate our life as part of our everyday language and images. We can see this in the words and symbols derived from gambling, which are commonly used in many situations, such as describing someone who is unpredictable as a "wild card", or giving advice by starting with "Your best bet is to..." Advertising is filled with references to gambling, with phrases such as "Best Deal" or "Blue Chip Quality." If you were to hear someone say, "For openers, I will increase the ante in this lawsuit and let the chips fall where they may. I refuse to stand pat and although I am being bluffed by that fourflusher, I will not reveal my ace in the hole until the showdown. His poker-faced lawyer expected us to fold but we are going to step up the action, raise the stakes and go for broke", you would understand that the person was talking about a lawsuit, although the passage contains thirteen terms derived from gambling with cards, especially poker.

Arising from our society's ambivalence about gambling, various political administrations in nearly every state and county of the country have created cycles of accepted legal gambling, followed by laws to make it illegal, followed by legalization, and so on. As Charles Cotton wrote in 1674 in *The Compleat Gamester* "For what to one is most pleasant, to another is most offensive." This cyclical process allowed many artifacts of gambling to accumulate in numerous locations across the country. Each time some form of gambling became illegal, the equipment was hidden or stored away, with hopes that it would again be used in the not too distant future. These are the antiques that collectors search for today. In addition, the equipment from games that lessened in popularity, or became outmoded and were replaced by more modern styles, may also be found by innovative collectors - sometimes in large quantities.

As you will discover throughout this book, there are a multitude of fascinating objects and artifacts that were used in many different types of gambling games, such as Pharo, Poker, Diana, Hazard, Roulette, Slot Machines, Craps, Chuck-a-Luck, Keno, Lotteries, Bingo, Horse Racing, Sports Betting, Black Jack, Wheels of Fortune, and many others.

Collectors of these gambling antiques and memorabilia are extremely interested in knowing the date when each article was made, and if possible they also want to know the source of its manufacture and how it was used. Once the origin, development, and the overall history of any game is understood, it makes each discovery that much more meaningful, like finding a missing piece of a jigsaw puzzle.

When I first became interested in gambling and the history of gambling in my early teen age years during the 1950s, I began to read many books on the subject, each one leading to many others. Learning about the history of gambling in the United States is intriguing because it so accurately reflects American history and the developments and changes in the attitudes, customs and lifestyles of Americans over a period of more than 350 years. The more you learn, the more it whets your curiosity, so that each object you discover might send you on a Sherlock Holmes quest for more details. Whether the game is gambling or gambling collectibles, the following is always true; the more you know, the better you'll do.

Finding the Monitor and Merrimac deck of playing cards which was manufactured in 1865, led me to read several books about the Civil War, a subject that had not been of particular interest to me before. Suddenly I had to understand why one of the Aces in the deck stated, "To commemorate the greatest event in naval history, the substitution of iron for wood." A tiny political button for Teddy Roosevelt that shows a design of Four Aces, encouraged me to read about the assassination of President McKinley in 1901 and how it affected the politics of our nation. Discovering the Pocahontas deck of 1906 motivated me to learn that Pocahontas had repeatedly led long processions of the Powhatan people with baskets of corn bread, deer, turkey and strings of fish, bringing these to the settlers of Jamestown. She saved the Jamestown colony from starvation in the winter of 1607/8. I also came across this grateful acknowledgement from Captain John Smith, leader of the colony, "Pocahontas preserved this colony from death, famine and utter confusion."

Acquiring a postcard photo of the gambling room in the Merchant's Hotel of Goldfield, Nevada, and one from a gambling saloon in nearby Tonopah, prompted me to take a cross country trip which included

HISTORICAL TOLL GATE SALOON AND GAMBLING HOUSE, BLACK HAWK, COLORADO

1940's Postcard of Toll Gate Saloon Realphoto of the historical Toll Gate Saloon and Gambling House that once flourished in Black Hawk, Colorado from the time of the 1870s. It was one of the gambling halls built in the heyday of gold mining and smelting in Black Hawk. The Toll Gate is once again a well-known name among the recently legalized gambling casinos of Black Hawk, Central City and Cripple Creek.

driving through central Nevada on the most deserted section of an interstate highway in the country. There I saw the remains and the efforts to rebuild those almost deserted silver and gold mining areas that had been boomtowns at the turn of the century. Another postcard with a photo of the original Toll Gate Gambling Saloon of Black Hawk, Colorado took me on a trip to Black Hawk and Central City, which filled me with a sense of nostalgia for those early pioneering days when pharo games were played with gold coins. Now, each time I read or hear some report of the recently relegalized gambling in both of those early Colorado mining towns, I look forward to visiting them again.

Along with those journeys across the country to absorb the feeling and history of gambling in frontier mining towns, searching for gambling antiques is always an exciting and pleasurable experience. Every trip to an antique show, flea market, auction, antique shop, or to other collectors to see what they have found, often with the hopes of trading, raises feelings of anticipation and the sense of adventure that is usually associated with going on a treasure hunt.

The treasure hunt by the collector for gambling antiques is often inspired by the expert craftsmanship that is apparent in so many of the articles. They were usually made of exotic or very fine woods such as ebony or rosewood and hand carved with ornate designs, or made of silver with breathtaking detail in the miniature images enamelled on them. Poker chips were frequently made of ivory, carefully cut and scrimshawed with unique designs. Gaming boxes that held cards and chips were often inlaid with fine woods, metals and mother-of-pearl in elaborate patterns and lined with satin or velvet. The meticulous detail and beauty on hand painted layouts for Pharo, Diana, and Roulette boards is surpassed only by the rare decks of individually hand painted cards. Because they were used in some very precise ways, some articles manufactured for various gambling games had to be constructed with great precision, perfectly balanced as in the case of a roulette wheel or a wheel of fortune, or exactly square as in the case of dice.

One of the most important factors in collecting gambling antiques and playing cards is the condition of each object or artifact. This means that the best condition is the one that is as close as possible to the condition at the time an article was first made. Each type or level of damage brings down the value dramatically, which is true in any type of antique collecting. However, some collectors do prefer to own certain types of gambling memorabilia whose use is more evident, feeling that they have a more authentic appearance. Over the decades, it has become apparent that items in excellent or mint condition continue to appreciate in value far more quickly than those which show more use or damage.

Many collectors focus in on one or a few specific areas within gambling collectibles. They might specialize in a particular field of gambling, such as pharo, poker, playing cards, slot machines, lotteries, horse racing, or ivory chips, or be interested in gambling antiques from a specific historic period such as the Civil War, or a combined specific historic period and geographic location such as the Early West. The collector of gambling antiquities can choose from a vast number of specialized areas, of which only a fraction can be shown in the limited space of a book. One collector I know limits his collecting just to different types of dice -- and has a vast collection.

Tastes and interests vary widely and this is what makes trading with other collectors possible. When you find an object that you know collector friends of yours have been searching for, you might also have found a way to acquire that deck or pharo casekeeper that they own, which you've been wanting. No matter what their specific focus might be, collectors of gambling antiques are also often "topical collectors," searching in other categories of memorabilia such as comic books, antique books, ephemera, paintings, songsheets, postcards, advertising, and Hollywood memorabilia, to find an item related to their particular gambling interest.

Modern casino collectibles and contemporary lottery tickets are already of interest. With the expansion and legalization of gambling in so many areas of the country, individuals are contacting each other through antique periodicals in order to buy, sell or trade items which are available to them locally, for similar items gathered by collectors in other locations.

Once you have been fortunate enough to acquire a precious gambling treasure, there are many ways to help protect and conserve it. It should be kept dust free and preferably in a cool dry space with as little sunlight as possible. All component parts should be kept together, whether the article is stored or displayed. Do not try to repair or improve an item, unless you are an expert at restoration, since this often leads to more harm than good. Be careful about the conservation materials you use, and never use rubber bands, labels or cellophane tape directly on an article. Every antique is naturally aging; the collector's aim should be to keep that gradual deterioration to a minimum by slowing down the process as much as possible.

It is helpful to keep a running inventory on each item that you add to your gambling collection, listing the date and source of your acquisition, the price paid, the value you believe it has, and anything unusual about it, especially condition. Keeping the document in your computer is wonderful but 3" x 5" index cards or a loose leaf notebook

Sitting Bull, 1901; Pocahontas, 1906; Buffalo Bill and Pawnee Bill, 1909
These three decks are a good illustration of how playing cards overlap into other collectible fields. These decks are of interest to playing card collectors, as well as to collectors of early Western memorabilia. All three were manufactured by the United States Playing Card Co. of Cincinnati, Ohio.

Left:
1911: National Soldiers' Home Postcard published exclusively for the Post Fund Store, National Soldiers' Home in Maine. An extremely poignant photograph of veterans of the Civil War, wearing parts of Union Army uniforms. Can you imagine the stories being told and retold about what they had experienced fifty years earlier, as they spend their senior years in "The Card Room" at this home for veterans.

Right:
1909: A Quiet Game Realphoto postcard of four young Native American men participating in a game on the Western Plains, taken by K.H. Martin. From the North American Post Card Co., Kansas City, Missouri. Native Americans were enthusiastic gamblers long before the arrival of Europeans in America. Extensive wagering was common on foot races, archery, lacrosse, and many other sports and games, some resembling card games.

Left:
1909: Gambling in Telluride Photo by J.C. Anderson & Co. This bar and gambling hall in Telluride, Colorado provides roulette, pharo and card games for its customers, as well as a cast iron wood burning stove, and the man with the star to maintain law and order. It was one of the 26 gambling saloons in Telluride at that time.

Below:
c. 1910: Red Heart Rum Ash Tray Depicted are four sure winning hands in the games of poker, bridge, pinochle and euchre, suggesting that the brand of Red Heart Rum in the center was also a sure winner. This 4.5" diameter metal ash tray was made for Henry White & Co. Distillers by American Art Sign Co. of Brooklyn, New York. This image of the four winning hands was very popular and was used by several different companies that made alcoholic beverages.

will also serve the purpose. As your collection grows larger, this inventory will help you remember what you have and the value you assigned to it. You might also want to update those values when you observe an identical or similar item being sold, but always keep a note of your original cost in money or trade. It is very helpful to note the name and address or phone number of the person who sold or traded the item to you. It will remind you of people who may be good sources for your specific areas of collecting, so that further correspondence and inquiries are possible. The list of contacts at the back of this book may also be helpful.

As I said before, all of life is taking chances. Taking a chance on collecting gambling antiques and memorabilia can provide you with both pleasure and profit. Once you learn to play this exciting game of collecting, the odds will be in your favor and you will soon become a sure winner.

Chapter One:
THIS IS POSITIVELY
THE LAST ROUND

The game of poker as it is so widely played today, originated in America, probably in New Orleans, during the early 1820s. Since that time it has gone through numerous transitions and continues to develop into new forms even in our own times.

However, poker is a game that had been evolving for a very long time. Most of the books written about poker trace its roots to early European card games such as Poque, Brag, Pochen, Primero, Ambigu, Brelan, Gilet, Post and Pair, and Bouillotte. Some of these games involved ranks of hands, board cards, betting, raising and even bluffing, but none were played with a 52 card deck and the five card hand. Although these ancestors of poker had many different names and rules, each had inherited certain characteristics from an ancient Persian [Iranian] card game called As-Nas.

Poker as an American institution is based upon the innovations applied by Yankee ingenuity to the games that were already popular, those brought from Europe to the young republic before 1820-1830. However, the straight, the draw, the flush, the royal flush, Jacks or Better, Five Card Stud, Seven Card Stud, High-Low, Hold-'Em, The Joker, Pot Limit, Freeze Out, Table Stakes and Unlimited Stakes -each developed in America.

In the early days of poker in America (1820-1830) it took a long time for changes to be nationally accepted. Even today changes occur gradually. As an example in the 1950s in Seven Card Stud, High-Low, a 6/4 (6, 4, 3, 2, Ace) was the best low, or perhaps a 7/5 (7, 5, 4, 3, 2). A player had to have six cards to "swing" (attempt to win high and low). Today in most Seven Card Stud, High-Low or other high-low type games, a "Wheel" or "Bicycle" (5, 4, 3, 2, Ace) is the best low and is also the lowest straight, which can be used as a high hand.

I mention this to explain that it took 20 to 40 years to make this one simple change and there are still a small percentage of games that play the "old fashioned" style. We can assume that, beginning in the early 1820s, changes in the rules took just as long, and probably longer, to spread across the miles and then be accepted. This would be especially true because there were specific variations played in the West, the South, and the East of what was then a rapidly growing country. In addition, communications and mobility were certainly a lot slower than they are today.

The first mention of poker, by that name, in worldwide literature occurred in 1836 in the American book *Dragoon Campaigns to the Rocky Mountains; A History of Enlistment, Organization, and First Campaigns of the Regiment of the United States Dragoons*. No author's name actually appears in the book, but poker historians believe that it was either James Hildreth or Wm. L. Gordon Miller. Whoever the author was, the book described poker as "A favorite game of cards at the south and west", suggesting that it was already commonly played. The reference was to 20 card poker, consisting of the Ace, King, Queen, Jack and ten of the four suits. The rank of hands was one pair, two pair, three of a kind, a full house, and four of a kind as the best.

The second printed reference to poker was in *An Exposure of the*

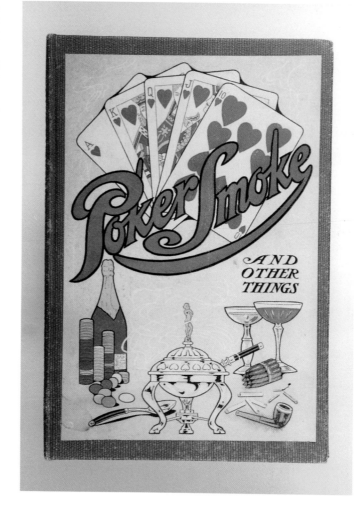

1907: Poker, Smoke and Other Things A 5.5" x 8" hardback book written by Percy Hammond and George C. Wharton, and published by Reilly & Britton Co. of Chicago. Numerous cartoon style illustrations in blue and orange ink are by Albert Olson. Written with a tongue in cheek style, they start out, "It is wrong to play poker--the way some men play it." Then claiming that poker was played even at the time of Adam and Eve, they humorously prove their assertion by saying, "The bible speaks of Cain 'raising his hand' against Abel."

Arts and Miseries of Gambling written by Jonathan H. Green, who referred to himself as "The Reformed Gambler". This book was published in 1843 by U.P. James of Cincinnati. It was the first book ever published in America which was written entirely about gambling, as well as the first book ever published in America to mention the word "gambling" in its title.

Green was the author of many books about gambling and cheating which were published between 1843 and 1859. One of the earliest dates for a game of poker being mentioned in any of Green's works was about a game in February of 1833. He described it as a 20 card game of poker on the Mississippi steamer Mohawk, which was traveling from Vicksburg to New Orleans. This was in his *Gambling Unmasked,* published by G.B. Zieber & Co. in 1847 (page 194). He also stated that "a flush is a legitimate hand in poker" (page 202), attesting to the origins of a flush in the early 1840s. In addition, Green mentioned a 52 card poker game as having been played on the Mississippi in 1837, but described it as a new innovation, and not generally known.

The first published poker rules appeared in an edition of *Hoyle's Games,* a book published by Henry F. Anners in Philadelphia in 1845. Both 20 card and 52 card poker were discussed, with the 52 card game being given much more attention. This shows that "full deck" poker was well on its way to replacing the 20 card game by 1845. (Incidentally, the original Hoyle whose name was used in so many later books of gaming rules, was Edmond Hoyle who actually lived between 1672 and 1769. He is the origin of the phrase "according to Hoyle" which means the correct way to do something.)

It was in the period of 1825-1840 that the great American game was born. They called it "Straight Poker" or "Bluff." It was played with a 52 card deck and was a serious and dangerous game. Each player received five cards, there was no draw, four aces was the best hand, and the game was played with unlimited stakes!!

I was astounded to discover that the original game involved unlimited stakes and that any player could bet whatever they had, including what was in their pockets or even in a nearby safe or bank. The player who was calling had 24 hours to produce the money but upon failing to do so, automatically forfeited all claims to the pot. (*Foster's Practical Poker* by R.F.Foster 1905, page 236; and *The Complete Poker Player* by John Blackbridge 1880, page 55)

These rules are explained in a well-known nineteenth century

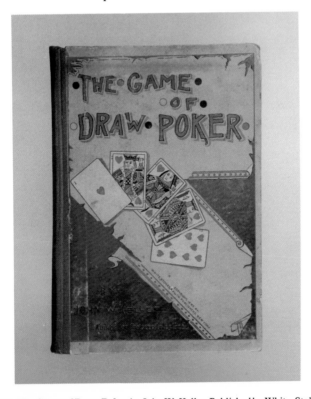

1887: The Game of Draw Poker by John W. Keller. Published by White, Stokes & Allen in New York. A paper label with gilt ink showing a royal flush, adorns the blue linen hardcover of this 4.5" x 6.5", 84 page book. It includes a ten page treatise by R.C. Schenck, and contains technical terms, mathematical probabilities and rules, along with other poker information.

poker tale about a gambler who took an envelope containing his hand of cards to a bank, hoping to secure a loan because all of his money was in the pot and he needed more to call a bet. A young bank teller turned him down, but when the president of the bank arrived just at that moment, peered into the envelope and saw four kings and an ace, he not only loaned the money to the man but returned to the game with him. When the game was over, the president of the bank advised the young teller that he should learn to play poker, and that a hand such as the one in the envelope was enough collateral on which to lend the entire assets of the bank. This story was the basis for a 1966 film with Henry Fonda entitled "A Big Hand for the Little Lady".

In the original game of Straight Poker or Bluff with unlimited stakes, there were two ways to begin. Either each player put up an equal amount, or the "buck" was used to designate whose turn it was to "ante" for the entire table. Each player received five cards and there was no draw. Starting at the dealer's left, each player either passed (meaning players could elect to hold their hands until a bet was made and then make a decision on their next turn) or bet any amount. When a bet was made, the next players, in turn, either folded (dropped out), stayed (called and continued to play), or raised any amount, until all had an equal amount in the pot.

The best explanation I have found about unlimited stakes is from *The Game of Draw Poker* by John W. Keller, published in 1887. "If two or more men agree to play the unlimited game, it is understood that each player is prepared to call any raise that any other player may make. If any player should make a bet to an amount greater than the sum of money immediately at the command of another player, and this second player should desire to call, the second player may have twenty-four hours in which to procure the money necessary to call the first player. In the meantime the cards are to be sealed up and lodged in hands satisfactory to both the players or all the players." (page 51). Keller goes on to say that the unlimited game, "...used to prevail on the Mississippi River steamboats...before the war, Southern planters were wont to stake untold gold, astonishing checks, whole plantations, and entire droves of Negro slaves, on the hands they held." (page 49).

By 1860, unlimited stakes had almost completely been replaced by table stakes with "sidepots." Each player was entitled to "a sight for his pile." This meant that when a player did not have sufficient chips to meet a bet or a raise, he could put all the chips he did have into the pot and call for "a sight for his pile." He would then wait until the end of the hand. At the conclusion of the hand, when all hands were shown, if the player who had called for "a sight for his pile" had the best hand, he could only win an amount from each player that was equal to the sum he had put into the pot. The next best hand was entitled to the balance of the pot, provided he had put in more money than the player who had called for "a sight for his pile." This concept continued until all money was removed from the pot.

In 1875, H.T. Winterblossom, in *The Game of Draw Poker Mathematically Illustrated*, wrote "The truth is, there is no science whatever necessary in the unlimited game, it is purely a question of intimidation. The limited game on the contrary is highly scientific." Unlimited stakes poker must have led to countless numbers of extremely interesting and dramatic scenarios and bluffs, many of which have been portrayed in American Western movies.

An early mention of poker in *Hoyle's Games* of 1845 states that it was played with a full deck of 52 cards, and that up to ten people could play. Since ten players would each have five cards, this conclusively shows that there was no draw in 1845. The idea of a draw of cards in poker started about 1850, along with betting limits. The first mention of "Draw Poker" in print is in *Bohn's New Handbook of Games* by Henry B. Bohn, published by Henry F. Anners of Philadelphia in 1850.

Draw Poker, although sometimes still played with unlimited stakes, was usually played with a limit agreed upon by all players before the game began. Since there were two rounds of betting, there

1895: It's All in the Draw by C.E.H. Brelsford and C.W. Dimick. Published by The Forbes Lithograph Mfr. Co. of Boston, Mass. This clever 5.5" x 9.5" book is made of ten sheets of hard cardboard tied with a braided cord laced through three holes, creating a 20 page book. As you open the book there is a limerick on each left hand page, and an illustration on the right hand side which visually supplies the last word or two of the limerick. On the left side of the next to last page we read, "Now 'tis late in the evening, and the biggest Jack Pot, all the chips on the table, are piled in one lot, silence has fallen, there's an expectant hush, they all faint as, you show this..." The right side shows a royal flush!

was usually a different limit for each round, such as ten dollars before the draw and twenty dollars after the draw. There was a limit also placed on the number of raises, generally agreed to be three per round.

The following terms were used in Draw Poker and are either obsolete or have an entirely new meaning in today's game. 1) The "Age" or "The Eldest Hand" was the player to the dealer's left, the one who put up the blind, usually one half of the first round limit. 2) The "Blind" was the amount put up by the "Age" before the cards were dealt. This was a compulsory bet. 3) The "Ante" was the amount each player equally contributed to the common pot to begin the game. Another definition from *The American Hoyle* published by Dick & Fitzgerald in 1864 was that "any bet in poker is called an ante." (page 175)

One of the most famous stories about the origin of a term in poker was that of the murder of James Butler Hickok (Wild Bill Hickok) by Jack McCall. It happened at a Draw Poker game in the Number Ten Saloon in Deadwood, South Dakota on August 2, 1876. Hickok, a well known lawman and professional gambler, was sitting at the game, but not in his usual seat which would have had his back against the wall. Vulnerable to the cowardly shot to the back of his head, Hickok fell to the floor, dropping his hand of two black aces, two black eights and a jack of diamonds. Since that day, a hand of aces and eights has been known as "The Dead Man's Hand".

Straights or sequences were introduced about 1855. In *The American Card Player* of 1866 we find, "It is strongly urged by some experts that the strongest hand in draw poker should be a straight flush, for the reason it is more difficult to get than four of a kind and removes from the game the objectionable feature of a known invincible hand. It is impossible to tie or beat four aces or four kings with an ace, but it is possible for four royal flushes to appear in the same deal. As no gentleman would care to bet on a sure thing, we therefore think that the straight flush should be adopted when gentlemen play at this game." [Dick & Fitzgerald, NY]

From *The American Hoyle*, "Straights are not considered in the game, although they are played in some localities, and it should always be determined whether they are to be admitted at the commencement of the game." In this 1864 edition are the first descriptions, in print, of the straight, the straight flush, the rules for draw poker, and an explanation of Five Card Stud, a poker game that did not become popular until 50 years later, and then remained very popular from about 1920 until 1955. In this 1864 edition, there is no mention of 20 card poker at all.

The straight was not nationally accepted until 1880. Books of this period warned players to ask if straights were played and if four aces was the best hand. When straights played so did straight flushes. The royal straight flush was decided upon as the best hand between 1865 and 1880. In the 1880 reprint of Blackbridge's 1875 *The Complete Poker Player*, he states that, "should a party of strangers open a poker game without making any mention of straights, they would not be valid."

It seems very likely that the Civil War of 1861-1865 was most responsible for the rise in popularity of poker and for developing some uniformity in the rules. Back then, as in the present time, poker was played with minor variations in different parts of the country. It is not hard to visualize poker being played by a vast number of soldiers of both the Union and the Confederate armies for many years during the war. The soldiers then took those experiences and rules back home with them to start "a little game with the boys." It seems that both the draw and the straight became widely accepted during that period.

Robert Cummings Schenck played a major part in standardizing the rules of poker. Schenck was a member of Congress from Ohio in the 1840s and the 1860s, Minister to Brazil in the 1850s, Brigadier General in the Union Army during the Civil War, and Minister to Great Britain from 1871 to 1876. However, among collectors of gambling antiques and those who love poker, he is better remembered as the "Father of Poker."

Schenck was a well known poker player in Washington, D.C., in the days when the capitol was known as the greatest poker playing town in the country. Herbert Asbury writes that Schenck engaged in many memorable poker sessions with Daniel Webster, Henry Clay, and other notable American statesmen. He was acknowledged as the best poker player in the United States. Perhaps he is most remembered for his "Poker Rules," printed in 1872, and his "Treatise on Poker," printed in 1875, both collating and explaining the rules of poker. These writings, especially the "Rules" written in 1872, made Schenck one of the most recognized authorities on poker during that period.

By the mid-1870s poker was becoming well known and increasingly widely played across America. This is strongly suggested by the almost simultaneous publishing of the first two books ever written exclusively about poker. These were *The Game of Draw Poker Mathematically Illustrated* by H.T. Winterblossom, published by Wm. A. Murphy, N.Y. 1875; and *The Complete Poker Player* by John Blackbridge, published by Advance Publishing Co., N.Y., 1875. Some

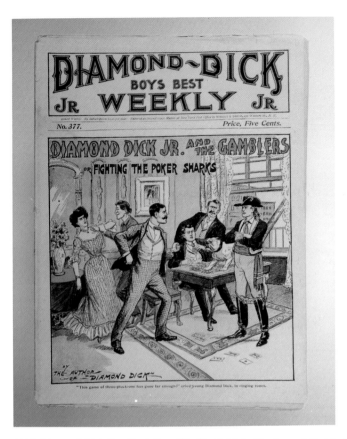

1904: Diamond Dick Jr.--Boy's Best Weekly Published by Street & Smith of New York on Jan. 2, 1904, issue No. 377. This early 8.5" x 11" pulp magazine for juvenile readers contains a 27 page story entitled "Diamond Dick Jr. and the Gamblers or Fighting the Poker Sharks."

poker historians believe that the Winterblossom book was the first known book to be written entirely about poker, basing their opinion on the statement, "Entered according to Act of Congress, in the year 1874, by William H. Murphy, in the Office of the Librarian of Congress at Washington" which was printed opposite the preface page. Others feel that the Blackbridge and Winterblossom books were written and published at about the same time, since there was no mention of the Library of Congress in the Blackbridge book at all.

In 1872 the game of Jackpots Poker was invented in Toledo, Ohio, another in a long line of innovations that added greatly to the popularity of the game. In Jackpots, all players contributed equal amounts to the pot before the cards were dealt. The betting could (optional) be opened by the player who held a pair of jacks or better. If no player qualified or chose to open, they "sweetened" the pot by all players again contributing equally, and then dealing again. It was not unusual for players to have contributed for three to six rounds before the pot was actually opened, often eliminating the effectiveness of a bluff.

For players who had been winning before the invention of Jackpots, the game became one of forced contributions. In their minds it destroyed the character of the game and reduced it to a lottery. According to Winterblossom, Jackpots was invented for the specific purpose of forcing "tight" or "close" players to come in more often. (Some things never change!) The game remained extremely popular for over 75 years.

The use of bucks became very intertwined with the invention of Jackpots. As I mentioned, bucks were used to designate the player whose deal or turn it was or for "ante" purposes. Bucks were originally knives with buckhorn handles or even a carved buckhorn itself, which is how the name originated.

In Draw Poker games, bucks were used to determine when a jackpot would be played. A game started with the buck in the center of

the table. The winner of the first pot then pulled in the buck along with the pot. Then on that winner's turn to deal he again placed the buck at the center of the table and announced a jackpot. The buck always passed to the winner of the pot, and the holder of the buck always dealt a jackpot. The surviving bucks today are very rare and are usually large pieces of ivory, scrimshawed with poker symbols, which evolved from the buckhorns.

By 1880, the rules of poker had become quite uniform and nationally accepted. Gone were hands such as those known as "The Blaze," "Little Dog," "Big Tiger," etc. The present rank of hands has remained the same from 1880 until today.

By the late 1880s, poker had become extremely popular. Richard Guerndale wrote in 1888, "The game of Draw Poker has often been called the national game of the United States and no game has a better claim to the title." He further explained that, "There is not a hamlet between the Atlantic and Pacific where the invitation to have a little game would not be instantly understood as an invitation to a game of Draw Poker. (*The Poker Book*, page 7) In 1896, Lieutenant F. Jarvis Patton wrote, "In the United States the game of Draw Poker is doubtless played more extensively than any game of cards the world over." (*How to Win at Draw Poker*, page 3)

By the end of the nineteenth century, approximately 50 books had been written about poker. Collecting poker memorabilia and especially antique poker chips has become one of the fastest growing of all collectible fields. Poker has left us a rich legacy of collectibles. Because the game was so popular, its image can be found on a great number of antiques, as well as on some very famous paintings. Ivory and clay poker chips, poker chip boxes, tables, books, bucks, and any artifact or image of the game are eagerly sought after by a rapidly growing number of collectors.

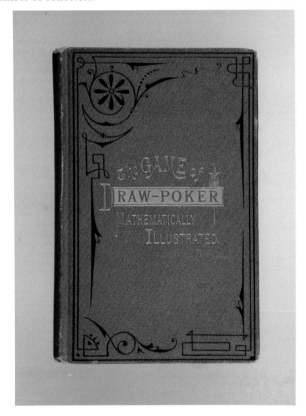

1875: The Game of Draw-Poker, Mathematically Illustrated by Henry T. Winterblossom, Professor of Mathematics Published by Wm. H Murphy of New York. Along with the first edition of Blackbridge's *Complete Poker Player*, published by Advance Publishing Co. in 1875, this 72 page, 4.5" x 6.5" book is one of the first two books written exclusively about poker. Winterblossom emphasized a discussion of the odds of drawing certain hands and the chances of improving the hand after the draw.

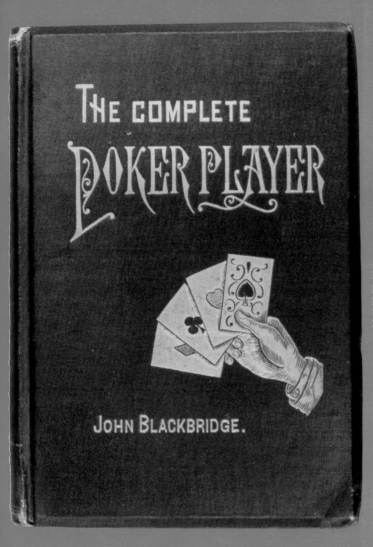

1880: The Complete Poker Player by John Blackbridge, a Counsellor of Law Published by Dick & Fitzgerald, New York. In this book Blackbridge refers to poker as "The National American Game." This 4.5" x 6" hardcover edition of 142 pages has a dark green linen cover imprinted with extremely well preserved intaglio gold printing of the title and image. The original edition of this book had 284 pages and was published in 1875 by Advance Publishing Co.

1880: The Complete Poker Player by John Blackbridge. A 4.5" x 6" soft cover book of 174 pages published by Fitzgerald Publishing Corp. of New York, successor to Dick & Fitzgerald. "A practical guide book to the American national game: containing mathematical and experimental analyses of the probabilities at DRAW POKER" is given as the subtitle on the title page.

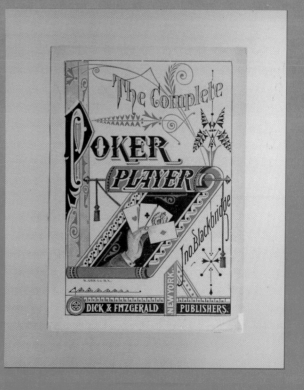

1896: Poker Chips, a Monthly Magazine Devoted to Stories of the Great American Game An entire set is seldom encountered, even in the most advanced collections. Each issue was covered with a bright and appealing art nouveau poker illustration and contained eight to twelve short stories that were about poker. These were said to be from "the most talented writers in the country," including John Chandler Harris of "Brer Rabbit" fame and Congressman Amos J. Cummings. Editor Frank Tousey wrote, "The stories will be interesting not only to poker players, but to all admirers of excellent fiction." Only six issues of this magazine were published, printed monthly between June and November of 1896. Tousey was also the publisher of this soft cover periodical, each 6" x 9.25" and consistently 60 pages, printed at North Moore Street in New York City. Five cents per copy, a price that always appeared on the cover as the value of a chip, or available through subscription at fifty cents per year.

Above:
Poker Chips, June, 1896, No.1 This is the first issue and has been found more than any of the others. At the back of the magazine, Tousey wrote a request for more manuscripts and explained that each would be "carefully read and if found suitable will be paid for liberally." On the last page was an ad for a bottle of Vino Kolafra addressed specifically to poker players. It claimed to be an antidote to alcohol, going on to say, "It's use INSURES A CLEAR HEAD and ABSOLUTE STRENGTH OF NERVE, two absolute essentials to a successful dalliance with the great American game."

Above right:
Poker Chips, July, 1896, No. 2 Tousey added a page with a subscription blank and another request for more manuscripts. The five cent chip here is marked "ante."

Right:
Poker Chips, August, 1896, No. 3 The five cent chip here is marked "limit." The cover depicts a Royal Flush in clubs, along with stacks of poker chips.

Poker Chips, September, 1896, No. 4 The phrasing on the cover changed from "stories of the great American game" to "original stories," perhaps reflecting Tousey's feeling that this might draw more readers. This issue also contains a more urgent request for stories. "A prize of $75 is offered by Poker Chips for the best original story, relating to any game into which the elements of luck or skill enters."

Poker Chips, November, 1896, No. 6 The last issue. This one included the prize winning story "The Iron Pot," a Civil War story about poker, by J. Irving Alden. In this issue, Mr. Tousey announced that his magazine would no longer be called "Poker Chips" but asked readers to look for the new title "The White Elephant" in December. He wrote that it would contain "poker and other stories relating to games of chance." Still hopeful, he promised a wider literary scope, listing such authors as Mark Twain, Bret Harte, A. Conan Doyle, Stephen Crane, and Rudyard Kipling. In 1896, Frank Tousey had a dream and tried to turn it into a reality; unfortunately it failed after six months. However, a century later, his dream has finally come true as collectors now hold his work in the highest esteem.

Poker Chips, October, 1896, No. 5 Contains a full page ad for the four back issues, listing each of the stories that had been included.

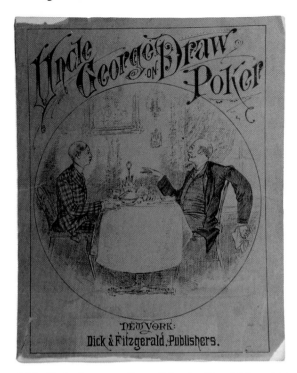

1883: Uncle George on Draw Poker by Wm. Brisbane Dick. Published by Dick & Fitzgerald of New York, this 50 page heavy paper cover book, was written in a familiar conversational manner as a lesson to his young nephew. "Uncle George" includes valuable suggestions about "this great American Game." There is an ad on the back cover for Blackbridge's 1880 edition of the *Complete Poker Player*. The paper cover edition was fifty cents; the clothbound, one dollar. 6" x 7.25".

1888: The Thompson Street Poker Club from *Life* Although not marked in the book, the author is believed to be Henry Guy Carleton. Published by White & Allen of New York, this 6" x 9" hardcover book has 48 pages. Pen and ink drawings by E.W. Kemble, who was a staff artist for *Life Magazine*, illustrate the story. Note the four aces falling out of the sleeve.

1888: The Mott Street Poker Club Although unmarked with an author's name, the author is believed to be Alfred Trumble. This 6" x 9" soft cover book of 50 pages was published by Dick & Fitzgerald in New York. Profusely illustrated with Michael Woolf's pen and ink drawings of a New York City poker club.

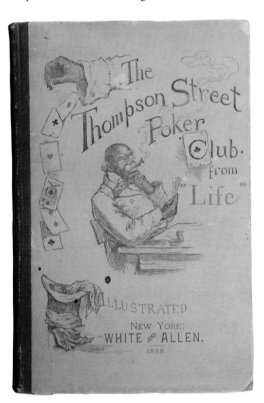

1888: The South Fifth Avenue Poker Club This soft cover, 5.5" x 8" paperback with 107 pages is an extremely rare book. The publisher is M.J. Ivers Co. of New York but the author is unknown. It is a novel about a poker club in late nineteenth century New York City with numerous pen and ink illustrations of the members of the club involved in poker activities.

c. 1880: Ivory Poker "Buck" The buck was an object used at the poker table to designate whose turn it was to deal or for ante purposes. This is the source of the phrases, "pass the buck" and "the buck stops here." The 2" x 2.25" buck is hand-scrimshawed with four aces and the words "Jack Pot," the name of an early form of poker developed in Toledo, Ohio in 1875.

Reverse Side of Ivory Poker "Buck" Hand-scrimshawed pot.

c. 1880: Ivory Poker "Buck" Spread of four aces and "You Deal" hand-scrimshawed on a 2.75" x 3" oval of ivory and filled in with both blue and red ink.

Reverse Side of Ivory Poker "Buck" A pot named "JACK" to symbolize the game of Jack Pot.

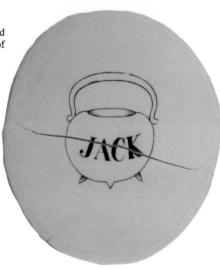

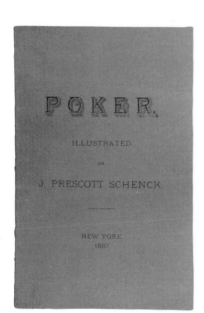

1887: Poker by J. Prescott Schenck. 8 page booklet, published in New York, with heavy paper cover and four beautifully done illustrations symbolizing card hands, printed on 4.75" x 7" thin board. He writes that poker is, "a necessary part of every man's education." and identifies himself as the President of the Thompson Street Poker Club. A tongue in cheek treatment, including, "Poker dates back to the ark, when Noah held two of a kind." Note that this is not Robert C. Schenck.

1887: Poker by J. Prescott Schenck. Two of the center page illustrations included in *Poker*. Although no artist is identified, these imaginative paintings were later used on several trade cards.

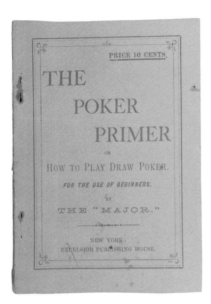

1886: The Poker Primer by "The Major." Published by Excelsior Publishing House of New York. This 31 page, 4" x 6" soft paper cover booklet contains rules and strategies for beginning poker players.

1889: Lectures by the Thompson Street Poker Club No author name is mentioned but this book is believed to have been written by Henry Guy Carleton. Published in New York by White & Allen, this 7.5" x 9" deluxe edition with gold and black intaglio printing on a rust colored linen hardcover has flowered endpapers. The 49 gilt edged pages contain numerous pen and ink sketches by J. Durkin.

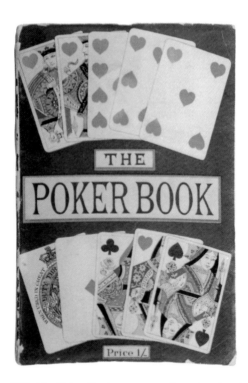

1889: The Poker Book by Richard Guerndale. Published by L. Upcott Gill in London. A paper cover showing a full house and a flush, on a 5" x 7.25" book of 80 pages. Illustrated with specific hands of cards in a poker game, it includes an explanation of how to play, technical terms, strategies and even a chapter on luck.

1888: The Police Gazette Card Player by "Jack Pot." Published by Richard K. Fox in New York. A 73 page, 5" x 6.5" pulp with a slightly out of register color printed circle of cards on soft paper cover. The hand-printing on the cover promises that it will explain how to play the seven games listed, starting with poker.

1892: Judge's Library - A Monthly Magazine of Fun, No.37 Judge Publishing Co. of New York. Possibly the only existent copy of this 36 page, 8" x 11" magazine. It is entirely devoted to poker. Filled with humorous poker related etchings and engravings by Zim, Hamilton, Ehrhart, J. Smith, L. Johnson and other fine artists of the day. A unique treasure.

c. 1890: Helps in the Game of Poker Author unknown. Published in New York by Patterson, Gottfried & Hunter, Ltd. This 16 page, 3.25" x 5.25", booklet has a paper cover with an art nouveau design featuring a royal flush in diamonds. It contains the rules and explanations of Draw Poker.

1903: How to Beat the Game by Garrett Brown. Published by G.W. Dillingham in New York. The color cover design is printed on the grey linen hardcover. 117 pages with twelve full page illustrations of very well done humorous watercolor paintings by Garrett Brown Jr. and Louis F. Grant, printed in black and white. Witty commentary on the poker scene, dedicated to "The Losers at Poker." 4" x 7"

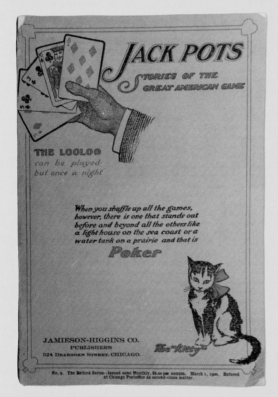

1900: Jack Pots--Stories of the Great American Game by Eugene Edwards. Published by Jamieson-Higgins Co. of Chicago. 5.25" x 7.5" soft cover book with 342 pages. It includes 24 short stories of poker games played in America and Europe with over 50 pen and ink illustrations by Ike Morgan. Note the tribute to poker on the cover.

1896: How to Win at Draw Poker by Lieut. F. Jarvis Patton. Published by Fitzgerald Publishing Corp. of New York. A 45 page, 4" x 6" booklet with heavy paper cover, it emphasizes mathematics and probabilities.

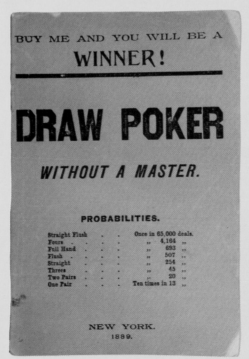

1889: Draw Poker Without A Master by Richard Guerndale. Published by G.W. Dillingham of New York. An 82 page, heavy paper cover, 5" x 7.25" book. The title page promises that this book will teach the reader, "How to play the fascinating game with success." It also includes "The authentic laws of the game."

1915: How to Play Poker by David A. Curtis Printed by Ogilvie Publishing Co. of New York. A 22 page, 3.5" x 5.5" paper cover booklet which discusses elementary rules for the games of Straight, Draw and Stud Poker.

c. 1910: Hoyle's Poker Primer Author and Publisher unknown. This 18 page, 5.25" x 7.5", soft paper cover booklet covers the popular poker games of the period. The last six pages are an expose of cheating at poker.

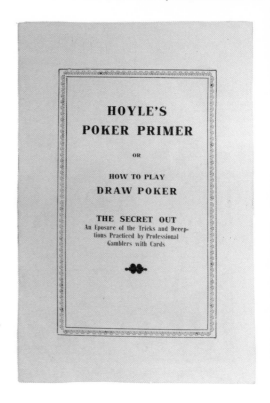

c. 1910: How to Win at Draw Poker A 22 page, 5.25" x 7.5" booklet published by Johnson Smith & Co. of Detroit. Author unknown. It covers the "laws of poker," the values of the hands, technical terms, and strategy for playing. The player was advised, "The main elements of success are, to quote Schenck, 'Good luck, good cards, plenty of cheek and good temper.'" The last seven pages are devoted to tips on how to avoid being cheated at the game.

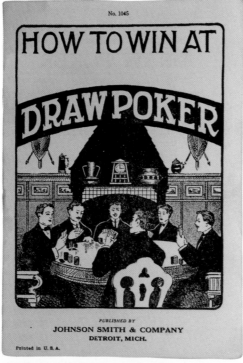

1913: The Poker Primer or How to Play Poker by "The Major." Published by Wehman Bros. in New York as part of their "Handy Series," this 4" x 5", soft cover booklet has 31 pages. This pulp publication includes a brief explanation of the rules and strategies of playing poker. Wehman also published small booklets on "Tricks With Cards," "Fortune Telling With Cards" and others in a similar vein, advertised at the back of this booklet.

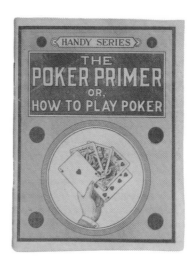

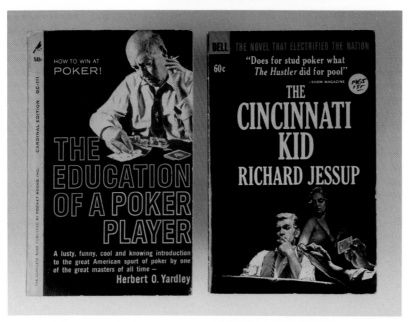

1960s: Two 60's Paperbacks on Poker   Left: *The Education of a Poker Player* by Herbert O. Yardley, was a 167 page Cardinal Edition by Pocket Books Inc., printed in 1961, originally copyrighted in 1957. A collection of humorous and informative poker stories that was "required reading" for a poker education at that time. Right: *The Cincinnati Kid* by Richard Jessup. The first paperback edition was by Dell, in April, 1965. It is a 158 page novel about two poker champions, each out to prove he was the best, which was made into a film starring Steve McQueen and Edward G. Robinson. I'm still wondering how Lancey (Robinson) could get a Straight Flush in Five Card Stud played with No Limit, especially when "The Kid" (McQueen) was on his way to making a full house. That's Hollywood!

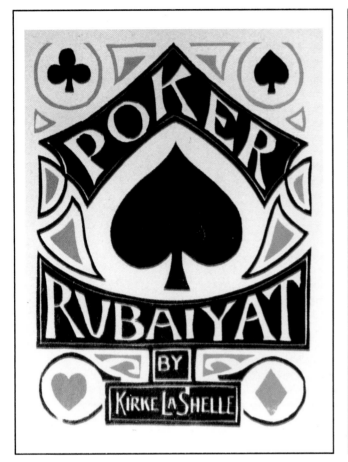

SURE-THING JOEY IN

1903: Poker Rubaiyat by Kirke La Shelle. Published by Bandar Log Press of Phoenix, Arizona. Above are two pages from the limited edition of 250 copies of this book. The format of this 28 page, soft cover book with 24 stanzas and 12 accompanying illustrations, is based upon the famous Rubaiyat of Omar Khayyam from medieval Persia. Each copy of the Poker Rubaiyat is composed of pages of handmade paper with actual woodcut prints done by artist Frank Holme. Bandar Log was the first private press to operate in the Territory of Arizona. A rare treasure!

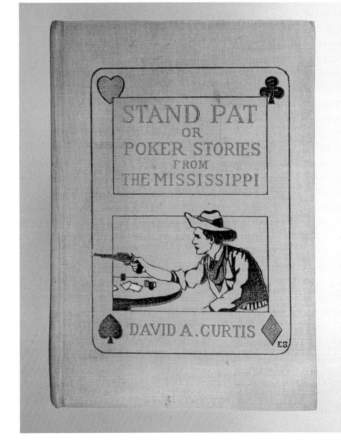

1906: Stand Pat, or Poker Stories from the Mississippi by David A. Curtis. Published by L.C. Page & Co. of Boston. Red and black intaglio printing on grey linen, adorn this 5.5" x 7.5" hardcover of 269 pages. The full page illustrations are black and white reproductions of paintings of gambling scenes by Henry Roth. 20 short stories of poker games on riverboats and in towns along the Mississippi.

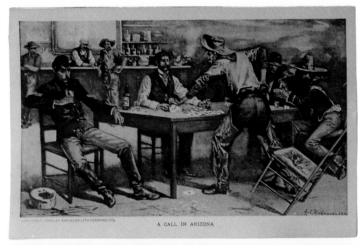

1909: Set of Poker Postcards This is one of six postcards reproduced from a set of six original lithographs of scenes that represent various types of people playing poker in different parts of the country. They were originally painted by five different artists and published by The Truth Co./American Lithograph Co. in 1895. The postcards were also printed by The American Lithograph Co. This one was titled, "A Call in Arizona," reproduced from a painting by A.C. Redwood. Note the Ace of Hearts on the floor and the Ace of Hearts on the table, leading to the player reaching for his gun.

1909: Set of Poker Postcards "A Showdown in the 400" The poker hand is about to conclude and the attention of the four players is riveted on the fifth man who is about to show his cards - the final "showdown." The illegible signature seems to be that of the same artist who painted "A Deal in Washington."

1909: Set of Poker Postcards "The Draw on the Bowery" The players are about to draw their cards in this game of Draw Poker in a room on the Bowery in New York City. Artist's signature illegible.

1909: Set of Poker Postcards "A Deal in Washington" If there are "deals" made anywhere, it's in Washington. Artist's signature is illegible.

A RAISE IN THE SOUTH

Opposite :
1909: A Sunday School Class in the West Postcard with color printing over photo by Charles E. Morris of Chinook, Montana. An eight-handed poker game with an armed guard at the door.

1909: Set of Poker Postcards "A Raise in the South" This print has also been known as "The Deacon Plants a Seed," referring to the player on the right who holds a Royal Flush and whose stack of chips is about to grow. Artist's signature is illegible.

1909: Set of Poker Postcards "A Bluff in Chicago" was painted by Thomas Strup. It features five gentlemen playing poker around a table with a large pot of chips at stake. Along with the images of drinking and smoking, we see cards strewn carelessly across the floor.

A BLUFF IN CHICAGO

693. A Navajo Poker Game, Arizona.   On the Santa Fe Ry.

c. 1905: A Navajo Poker Game Postcard from Arizona. A watercolor painting from along the Santa Fe Railway, printed as a postcard from Williamson Haffner Co. of Denver Colorado.

Below left:
1908: Western Gambling Room Photo postcard published by M. Rieder of Los Angeles. Unlike other gambling halls that have various types of gaming tables, this one seems to be set up entirely for poker.

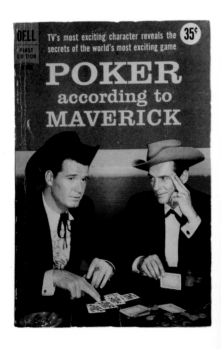

1959: Poker According to Maverick by "Bret Maverick." Published by Dell Publishing Co. of New York. 159 page paperback. This quote appears on the title page. "One thing Pappy told me was, 'If you know poker, you know people; and if you know people, you got the whole dang world lined up in your sights.'"

POKER ALICE:
The Legend Lives On

Poker Alice was born in Sudbury, England, on Feb. 17,1851. She arrived in America as a child and was educated in the United States. During her 79 years, she became widely known as a hard playing, quick shooting, winning pharo and poker player throughout the mining towns of Colorado, New Mexico, Arizona, and especially in Deadwood, Sturgis, and the Black Hills of South Dakota.

Poker Alice's various names were Alice Ivers, Alice Duffield, Alice Tubbs, and Alice Huckert. These were not aliases; they were her names before and during her three marriages. She married Frank Duffield, a Lake City, Colorado mining engineer when she was in her twenties but when he was killed in a mining accident, Alice was left to fend for herself. She started gambling at pharo and poker and was soon considered to be a professional at both games. Not long after, she became a pharo dealer and began to be continually on the move to the mining boom towns where the action was. Hardened professional gamblers liked to play at her table.

In 1907, she married a rival gambler in Deadwood, W.G. Tubbs. When Tubbs died of pneumonia after three years, she was heard to say that he was the only man she had ever really loved and she grieved this loss deeply. Her third marriage was to George Huckert in Sturgis, in the Black Hills of South Dakota, about 1913. Together, they opened a gambling and dance hall in Sturgis.

According to those who knew her, Alice was extremely self reliant and independent and known for keeping her promises. As an expert markswoman, she explained, "I always carried a gun and was never afraid." Although she claimed that she had only drawn her gun a few times, she did use it. She wounded one man while gambling and killed another in a non-gambling related incident. The latter shooting resulted in her being tried for murder, but she was found not guilty by reason of self-defense.

In an occupation where very few become famous, Poker Alice became a legend. Throughout many areas of the West, Poker Alice was known for being extremely honest and for being one of the winning gamblers. Asking no favors because of her gender, she met men on an equal footing. She was a religious woman and refused to work or gamble on Sunday. When she was asked in her somewhat poor, but proud seventies whether she had won or lost over the years, her eyes closed to a narrow squint. She bit down on her black cigar, and replied, "I never saw anyone get humpbacked carrying away the money they won from me."

Poker Alice was buried in the Catholic cemetery in Sturgis, South Dakota on February 27, 1930.

ANTIQUE POKER BOOKS:
1836 -1941
(in chronological order)

1836: The first printed reference to poker by that name was in the 1836 American book *Dragoon Campaigns to the Rocky Mountains*, believed to be written by James Hildreth, although some historians believe the author was Wm. L. Gordon Miller.

1843: The second mention of poker in print was in the 1843 book *An Exposure of the Arts and Miseries of Gambling* by Jonathan Harrington Green.

1845: The first printed mention of poker in a "Hoyle" was in *Hoyle's Games* in 1845.

1850: Draw Poker was first referred to in 1850 by Henry B. Bohn.

1864: The first printed reference to Stud Poker and a straight, along with the first printed rules for Draw Poker, was by "Trumps" *American Hoyle* in 1864. *All of these books and authors are more fully described in the introduction to poker.*

1872: The first printed poker rules in England were written by General Robert Cummings Schenck, the United States Minister to England. He introduced poker to the guests at a country home at Somersetshire. The hostess, a Duchess, persuaded Minister Schenck to write down the rules. In 1872, the Duchess privately printed and distributed these rules of poker for her court. The game caught Queen Victoria's fancy and the popularity of poker spread throughout Great Britain where it became known as "Schenck Poker".

1875: Blackbridge, John. *The Complete Poker Player.* New York, Advance Publishing Company, 284 pages.

1875: Schenck, R.C. "Draw Poker," published for the trade, 8 pages.

1875: _____. "Rules For Playing Draw Poker," reprinted from February 8, 1875, *New York Tribune*, 12 pages. (Neither of the 1875 Schenck publications are regarded as books.)

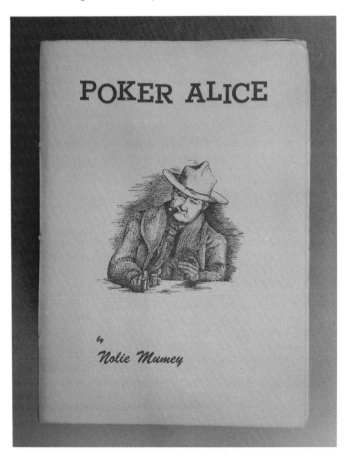

1951: Poker Alice by Nolie Mumey. Published by Artcraft Press of Denver, Colorado. 47 page, 8" x 11", paper board binding. The title page announces, "History of A Woman Gambler in the West." This book was dedicated to "All women who liked to gamble."

1875: Winterblossom, Henry T. *The Game of Draw Poker Mathematically Illustrated.* New York, W. H. Murphy, 72 pages.

1877: "A Professor" [Meehan, C. H. W.]. *Laws and Practice of the Game of Euchre and of Draw Poker.* Philadelphia, T.B. Peterson & Bros., 144 pages.

1879: Percy, Alfred. *Poker: Its Laws and Practice.* Allahabad, India. Pioneer Press.

1880: Blackbridge, John. *The Complete Poker Player.* New York, Dick & Fitzgerald Publishers, 142 pages, hardcover.

1880: _____. *The Complete Poker Player.* Fitzgerald Publishing Co., successor to Dick & Fitzgerald, 174 pages, softcover.

1880: Schenck, Robert Cummings. *Rules for Playing Poker.* Brooklyn, New York. Privately printed, 17 pages.

c. 1880: _____. *Draw Poker.* Published for the trade, 8 pages.

1881: Abbott, Jack. *Treatise on Jack Pot Poker.* New Orleans, Clark & Hofeline, 64 pages.

1882: Welsh, Charles. *Poker, How to Play it.* London. Griffith & Farren, 109 pages.

1882: Author Unknown. *Poker: The Rules of Poker.* London, Harrison, 16 pages.

1883: Dick, Wm. Brisbane. *Talks of Uncle George to His Nephew About Draw Poker.* New York, Dick & Fitzgerald, 50 pages.

1883: Proctor, Richard A. *Poker Principles and Chance Laws.* New York, Dick & Fitzgerald, 32 pages.

1884: Carleton, Henry Guy. *The Thompson Street Poker Club New York*, *Life* Magazine Publishers, 62 pages.

1884: Author unknown. *Draw Poker and Spoil Five.* London, Routledge & Sons.

1886: Gilkie, Robert J. *Experimental Drawing at Poker From Five Thousand Hands.* Dorchester, Massachusetts, publisher unknown, 13 pages.

1886: Gray, E. A. *Hints on Poker*, Cincinnati, Ohio, E.A. Gray & Co. 16 pages.

1886: "The Major". *The Poker Primer.* New York, Excelsior Publishing House, 49 pages.

1886: Phillips, Barnett. *The Poker Primer: Or How to Play Draw Poker.* New York, Excelsior Publishing Co., 31 pages.

1887: Debian, Dennis. *The Game of Draw Poker.* New York, White & Allen. 25 pages.

1887: Dick, W. B. *Progressive Poker.* New York, Dick & Fitzgerald.

1887: _____. Another edition of Dick's *Progressive Poker*, this one 8" x 11", containing Schenck's rules.

1887: Keller, J.W. *The Game of Draw Poker.* New York, White, Stokes & Allen, 84 pages.

1887: MacKenzie, Collins. *Jack-Pots: Poker Stories.* Chicago, Illinois, The Illustrated Publishing Co., 160 pages.

1887: Proctor, R.A. *Chance and Luck With Notes on Poker.* London, Longmans, Green & Co., 263 pages.

1887: Schenck, Prescott J. *Poker Illustrated.* New York, publisher unknown, 8 pages.

1887: Author unknown. *Science in Poker.* New York, G.W. Dillingham,

1888: Carleton, Henry Guy. *Thompson Street Poker Club.* New York, Dick & Fitzgerald, 49 pages.

1888: Guerndale, R. *Draw Poker Without a Master.* London, The Bazaar Office.

1888: Carleton, Henry Guy. *The South Fifth Avenue Poker Club.* New York, Ivers & Co., 107 pages.

1888: Carleton, Henry Guy. *The Thompson Street Poker Club From Life.* New York, White & Allen, 48 pages.

1888: Trumble, Alfred. *The Mott Street Poker Club.* New York, White & Allen, 50 pages. (Also printed by Wm. Paterson, Edinburgh and by Dick & Fitzgerald, New York in the same year)

1889: Guerndale, R. *Draw Poker Without a Master.* New York, G.W. Dillingham, 82 pages.

1889: Guerndale, Richard. *The Poker Book.* London, L. Upcott Gill, 80 pages.

1889: Laugher, A.B. *Poker.* London, publisher unknown, 28 pages.

1889: Author unknown. *Lectures Before the Thompson Street Poker Club.* New York, White & Allen, 49 pages.

1889: Pardon, C.F. [Rawdon Crawley]. *Poker.* London, Chas. Goodall & Sons.

1890: Henry, R.J. *Poker Boiled Down...* Boston, Tourist Publishing Co., 13 pages.

1892: Editor unknown. *Judge's Library: A Monthly Magazine of Fun ("All About Poker")*, No. 37, April, 1892, New York, Judge Publishing Co., 36 pages.

1892: Florence, W.J. *Gentlemen's Handbook on Poker*. London, Routledge & Sons, 195 pages.
1892: Hoffman, Wm. *Draw Poker: The Standard Game*. London, Routledge & Sons, 115 pages.
1895: Allen, G.W. *Poker Rules in Rhyme*. New York and St. Louis, publisher unknown, 74 pages.
1895: Brelsford, C.E.H. and Dimick, C.W. *It's All in the Draw*. Cincinnati, Ohio, The Russell & Morgan Printing Co., 20 pages.
1895: Cady, Alice Howard. *Poker: The Modern Game*. New York, American Sports Publishing Co., 37 pages.
1895: Templar. *The Poker Manual*. London, Mudie & Sons, 119 pages.
1896: Lillard, J.F.B. *Poker Stories...* New York, Harper Bros., 251 pages.
1896: Patton, Lieut. F.J. *How to Win at Draw Poker*. New York, Fitzgerald Publishing Corp., 45 pages.
1896: Tousey, Frank, ed. *Poker Chips: A Monthly Magazine*. New York, Published by Frank Tousey (Issues from June, July, August, Sept., Oct. & Nov.).
1897: Carleton, Henry Guy. *Lectures Before the Thompson Street Poker Club*. New York, J. Parker White, 49 pages.
1897: Foster, R.F. *Poker*. New York, Brentano's, 104 pages.
1897 Author Unknown. Decisions on Moot Points of Draw Poker. New York, New York Consolidated Card Co.
1900: Curtis, David A. *Queer Luck: Poker Stories*. New York, Brentano's, 235 pages.
1900: Edwards, Eugene. *Jack-Pots*. Chicago, Jamieson-Higgins & Co., 342 pages (soft & hardcover editions).
1901: Curtis, David A. *The Science of Draw Poker*. New York, self-published, 216 pages.
1901: Reynolds, Alleyne. *Poker Probabilities Calculated*. Sheffield, U.K., Paulson & Brailford, 40 pages.
1901: Templar. *The Poker Manual*. London, F. Warne, 119 pages.
1901: Author unknown. *The Laws of Poker*. London, The Cleveland Club.
1902: Abbott, Jack. *A Treatise on Jack Pot Poker*. New Orleans, Geo. Muller & Co., 64 pages.
1902: Hirst, E. def. *Poker as Played by Skilled Professional Gamblers*. Publisher unknown.
1902: Edwards, Eugene. *Ante-I Raise You Ten*. Chicago, Jamieson-Higgins, 342 pages.
1903: Brown, Garrett. *How to Beat the Game*. New York, G.W.Dillingham, 117 pages.
1903:Florence, W.J. *Handbook on Poker*. London, Routledge & Sons, 195 pages.
1903: La Shelle, Kirke *Poker Rubaiyat*. Phoenix, Arizona, Bandar Log Press, 28 pages.
1903: McCarty, Robert A. *Poker, A Reflection on the Game*. Self-published.
1904: Foster, R.F. *Practical Poker*. London, Thos. De La Rue, 252 pages.
1904: Philpots, E.P. *A Treatise on Poker*. London, Simpkin & Marshall, 93 pages.
1905: Foster, R.F. *Practical Poker*. New York, Brentano's, 253 pages.
1905: Fox, Richard K. *Poker: How to Win*. New York, Richard K. Fox Publisher, 90 pages.
1905: Ritter, F.R. *Advantage Card Playing and Draw Poker*. Publisher unknown, 117 pages.
1906: Ballard, Martha C. *Shakespeare on Poker*. Denver, Colo. Ballard Publishing Co., 24 pages.
1906: Curtis, David A. *Stand Pat or Poker Stories from the Mississippi*. Boston, Massachusetts, L.C. Page & Co., 269 pages.
1907: Hammon, P., Wharton, G.C. *Poker, Smoke, and other Things*. Chicago, Illinois, Reilly & Britton, 69 pages.
1909: "Jackpot". *Poker-Patience*. International Card Co., 20 pages.
1909: "Retired Card Sharp". *How to Win at Draw Poker Scientifically...* Philadelphia, Pennsylvania, Royal Publishing Co., 119 pages. [Two other editions same year: Philadelphia, Crawford & Co., 119 pages; Cleveland, Arthur Westbrook & Co., 119 pages.]
1910: Foster, R.F. *Pocket Laws of Poker*. London, Thos. De La Rue.
1912: Fox, Richard K. *Poker; How to Win*. New York, Fox Publishing.
1912: Hoffman, Wm. *Draw Poker: The Standard Game*. Toronto, Musson Book Co., 115 pages.
1913: Hoffman, W. *Draw Poker: The Standard Game*. Dutton
1913: Laugher, A.B. *Poker*. London, Chas. Goodall, 28 pages.

1913: "The Major". *The Poker Primer or How to Play Poker*. New York, Wehman Bros., 31 pages.
1913: Phillips, Barnett. *The Poker Primer or How to Play Draw Poker*. New York, Platt & Peck Co., 31 pages.
1914: Hardison, Theodore. *Poker; A Work Exposing...* St. Louis, Missouri, Hardison Publishing Co., 120 pages.
1914: Hoffman, Wm. *Draw Poker-The Standard Game*. London, Routledge & Sons, 115 pages.
1915: Crofton, A. *Poker: Its Laws and Principles*. New York Wycil & Co., 92 pages.
1915 Curtis, David A. *How to Play Poker...* New York, Ogilvie Publishing Co., 22 pages.
1915: Underwood, Drury. *Chips That Pass in the Night*. Chicago, Illinois, The Howell Co.
1915: Author Unknown. *How to Play Poker*. Made by United States Playing Card Co., New York, Ogilvie Publishing Co., 22 pages.
1916: Brown, Garrett. *The Autocrat of the Poker Table or How to Play the Game to Win*. Boston, Massachusetts, R.G. Badger, 105 pages.
1916: DeWitt, E.F. *Hubbard on Poker*. Publisher unknown, 27 pages.
1916:"Hoyle" (pseudonym). *How to Play Poker*. New York, Ogilvie Publishing Co.
1916: Lorsch, Edwin S. *The Autocrat of the Poker Table*. Publisher unknown, 105 pages.
1921: Harper, Henry Louis. *How to Beat Draw Poker*. St. Louis, Missouri, self-published.
1921: _____ . *How to Beat Stud Poker*. St. Louis, Missouri, self-published.
1923: Heineman, Walter Raleigh. *Draw Poker*. New York, Chrisholm Printing Co., 48 pages.
1925: Kerfax, P.O. *Seveare's Record of 40,000 Poker Hands*. Self-published.
1925: Smith, Russell A. *Poker to Win*. El Paso, Texas, publisher unknown, 110 pages.
1925: Webster, Harold Tucker. *Webster's Poker Book...* New York, Simon & Schuster, 126 pages. [Two editions in hardback, one with separate compartment containing cardboard poker chips and I.O.U.'s.]
1928: Strong, Julian. *How to Play Poker*. New York - London, W. Foulsham, 64 pages.
1928: Author unknown. *Poker as it was Played in Deadwood in the Fifties*. Palo Alto, California, Wheatstalk Press, 5 pages.
1929: Allan, L. *The Laws of Poker...* Publisher unknown, 41 pages.
1929: Arnold and Johnston. *Poker*. London, Routledge & Sons, 166 pages.
1929: Bergholt, Ernest.*A Compendium of Poker*. London, Goodall & De La Rue, 38 pages.
1931: Fisher, G.H. *How to Play Stud Poker*. Gerard, Kansas, Haldemen-Julius Publishing Co., 63 pages.
1933: _____.*How to Win at Stud Poker*. Los Angeles, California, Stud Poker Press, 111 pages.
1934: Ellinger, M. *Poker*. London, Faber & Faber, 189 pages.
1934: Fisher, G.H. *Stud Poker Blue Book*. Los Angeles, California, Stud Poker Press, 111 pages.
1935: Carle, Richard. *What I Know About Poker*. Chicago, Illinois, Darrow Printing Co.
1938: Wickstead, James M. *How to Win at Stud Poker*. Louisville, Kentucky, Stud Poker Publishing Co., 101 pages.
1939: Author Unknown. *Win at Poker*. New Orleans, Louisiana, Crescent Publishing Co.
1940: Jacoby, Oswald. *Oswald Jacoby on Poker*. New York, Doubleday, Doran & Co., 155 pages.
1940: "King, Jack". *Confessions of a Poker Player*. New York, I. Washburn, Inc., 209 pages.
1941: Patton, F. Jarvis. *How to Win at Draw Poker...* New York, Wehman Bros., 45 pages.
1941: Author unknown. *Poker, Official Rules...* Cincinnati, Ohio, United States Playing Card Co., 64 pages.

Uncertain Chronology:
c. 1890: Author Unknown. *Helps in the Game of Poker*. New York, Patterson, Gottfried & Hunter Ltd., 16 pages.
c. 1910: Author Unknown. *Hoyle's Poker Primer or How To Play Draw Poker*. Chicago, J.C. Dorn, 18 pages.
c. 1910: Author Unknown. *How to Win At Draw Poker*. Detroit, Michigan, Johnson Smith & Co., 22 pages.

THE QUEEN OF SPADES.

THE QUEEN OF DIAMONDS.

THE QUEEN OF CLUBS.

THE QUEEN OF HEARTS.

Chapter Two:
ONE PICTURE IS WORTH A THOUSAND WORDS

This chapter is a visual history of gambling as portrayed on antique photographs and postcards. The images range from Western frontier gambling saloons to offshore gambling ships to elegant European casinos, and vary from humorous to serious visual commentaries on gambling. Offering us a broad view of gambling from bygone eras, these pictures often show what are now valuable gambling antiques, as well as being treasured collectibles themselves. I have kept this introduction short since each picture speaks volumes.....

Gambling Raid in New Orleans, May 12, 1954 This photo was taken in the "188 Gambling Casino" in Arabi, a suburb of New Orleans. The Louisiana State Police were taking the names and addresses of the people who had been breaking the law by playing there.

Opposite:
1909: Moffat Yard Postcards This set of four Queens done in pastels chalk by Will Grefe, and printed by Moffat, Yard & Co. of New York, shows four young woman whose hairdos are styled in the shapes of each of the four suit signs. These same four images were also beautifully printed on delicate pebble paper as a set of 12.5" x 17" posters in the same year.

c. 1910: **Early Days in Tonopah Postcard** Published by Newman Post Card Co. of Los Angeles. The photo on this card shows a bar and restaurant in Tonopah, Nevada, a silver and gold mining town about 20 miles north of Goldfield. The four men at the table play cards near the stove that provided warmth in the cold mountain winters.

1905: A Thirst Parlor in a Nevada Mining Camp Photo postcard by Frank H. Leib of Salt Lake City. Tables of poker playing miners sit in front of an advertising sign from Anheuser Busch of St. Louis. The rough saloon with a broad wooden planked floor and open beams appears to have been erected rather hurriedly to keep the men occupied.

c. 1900: **Where All Men Are Equal** Postcard photo from Detroit Publishing Co. The men are gathered around a game of craps with an old fashioned layout on the table. Note sign on left wall, "THESE DICE GUARANTEED - to be SQUARE"

c. 1900: **Oregon Indians Pastime** A postcard photo with a rude, stereotypical subtitle on the card. The group, seated on a blanket near a tepee, play a quiet game of cards. Published by Louis Scheiner in Portland, Oregon.

c. 1905: Navaho Indians Gambling in Arizona from Detroit Publishing Co. The sandy desert provides a comfortable setting for this intriguing card game. The interested spectators include a small child. Photograph by Fred Harvey, well known for his printing and illustrations.

c. 1905: Mojave Indians Gambling from Needles, California. Another Fred Harvey postcard photo depicting a group of Native Americans, mostly women, participating in a card game on the Mojave Desert. Detroit Publishing Co.

c. 1900: Roulette Postcard Realphoto. In an effort to bring the latest innovations to America, these entrepreneurial fellows erected a carnival-like tent with a sign announcing, "Roulette, Latest Craze." This introduction to roulette cost ten cents.

c. 1905: A Roulette Game in the West Photo postcard by M. Rieder, Publisher in Los Angeles. Printed on the back of the card, "$20,000 of gold in sight," referring to the stacks of gold coins on the table.

1910: Roulette Postcard Realphoto of a roulette game in an unidentified western town, the mud and dust on the shoes of the players suggesting that in this frontier town, sidewalks had not yet been built. Note unusually tall stacks of chips on the table and the two spittoons on the floor.

Early 1900s: Nevada Roulette Game Realphoto postcard by Osborn of the G. & K. Drug Co. of Rawhide, Nevada. A roulette game in progress.

~ Evans' De Luxe Roulette Wheel ~

Page 6

~ Evans' De Luxe Roulette Wheel ~

THIS is a Custom Built Roulette Wheel, regulation size, ornamented and embellished to meet the requirements of the exclusive Club; a Wheel with beauty of design and performance unequalled. The construction of the wheel is identical with that of the Regulation Roulette Wheel as described on page 2, in all respects except as to veneers and finish.

In designing the Evans' De Luxe Roulette Wheel, the markets of the world were searched for the rare and beautiful woods that enter into the makeup of this wheel and the artistry displayed in the inlays and striping is unexcelled. The Wheel and Bowl

are artistically inlaid, striped and divided with imported German marquetry of special design, individually worked out.

The Center Ornament as illustrated is distinctive, showing a miniature statue of the Goddess of Chance surmounting an ornamental center piece. This is a radical departure from the time honored Roulette Head and adds considerably to the artistic beauty and individuality of the De Luxe Wheel. No detail however small has been overlooked in making this wheel a superlative piece of Casino equipment. We also furnish this wheel with the conventional style head when preferred.

No. 20F247 Evans' De Luxe Roulette Wheel ....Each $250.00

Page 7

1935: Evans Catalog Pages 6 & 7 offer their custom built deluxe roulette wheel for $250.

c. 1920: Juarez Postcard Central Cafe in Juarez, Mexico. The wall on the right is lined with slot machines, including three older floor models from the early 1900s. The machine in the middle appears to be a 1905 Cricket by Mills Novelty Co. of Chicago.

1929: Juarez Postcard Central Cafe in Juarez, Mexico. This photo, taken from the other end of the room, shows that a decade later, the floor machines have been removed. Hopefully, some lucky collector has that Mills' Cricket.

Early 1930s: Juarez Postcard A Realphoto postcard from the Cafe Mint Restaurant in Juarez, Mexico. Note that the wall opposite the bar is lined with slot machines. Juarez is just across the Rio Grande River from El Paso, Texas and was one of the border towns which had legal slot machines, along with other activities that were illegal in most of America.

Early 1930s: Juarez Postcard Realphoto of the Gem Bar in Juarez, Mexico, which advertises itself as "The Home of Good Cheer." Customers are raising a toast, perhaps to the friendly relationship between the U.S. and Mexico, as symbolized by the crossed flags of both countries.

Early 1930s: Juarez Postcard Realphoto of the San Louis Bar photographed by Angel. Three "War Eagle" slot machines were available to customers for five cent or twenty-five cent play. The "War Eagles," with a large stylized brightly colored eagle on the front, were made by Mills Novelty Co. of Chicago between 1931 and 1944.

Early 1930s: Juarez Postcard Realphoto by W.H. Horne of El Paso, Texas. This scene of the "Monte Carlo" gambling hall in Juarez, shows a deluxe model Chuck-a-Luck cage with three large dice and a decorative eagle perched on top. Note the painted table layout. According to the sign on the wall, "Smallest bets taken $0.25; No action on cock dice." (dice not landing flat)

1931: Postcard from Reno A Realphoto of four women playing at the crap table at the Willows Casino in Reno, Nevada. Note the elegant decor.

1931: Postcard from Reno A Realphoto of three women playing Chuck-a-Luck at the Willows Casino in Reno, Nevada.

1931: Postcard from Reno A Realphoto of a group of women at the roulette table in Willows Casino, Reno Nevada. Note that the woman standing next to the croupier is the same woman as in the crap table photo.

1931: Postcard from Reno A sepia-toned Realphoto of a group of players posing at the roulette table in the Owl Club in Reno, Nevada. Note the simpler decor and the less formally dressed customers, as contrasted with the photos of the Willows Casino.

1932: Postcard from Reno A Realphoto postcard from the Waldorf in Reno, Nevada. Note the c. 1930 "Superior" slot machines manufactured by Caille Bros. of Detroit that are placed directly on the bar, alongside the c. 1905 Mills "Commercial" Trade Stimulator. A 1907 "Centaur" floor model slot machine, also from Caille, is at the lower right.

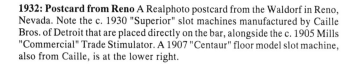

Early 1930s: Postcard from Reno A Realphoto of the Silver Slipper Casino in Reno, Nevada. Note roulette, craps and Black Jack tables.

Late 1930s: Postcard from Reno A Realphoto of the roulette tables at the Bank Club, Reno, Nevada.

1910: Illinois Smoke Shop Postcard Realphoto. Two trade stimulators are on the counter of this well-stocked tobacco shop in Carpentersville, Illinois. The machine on the left is an ornately cast iron c. 1905 "Puritan" made by Puritan Machine Co. of Detroit. The one on the right is an equally ornately cast iron c. 1906 "HY-LO" from Caille Bros. of Detroit. The little "Puritan" was conveniently located directly in front of the cash register, tempting customers to take a chance with a few coins from their change.

1905: Winnemucca Saloon Postcard A Realphoto postcard of the "Up To Date Saloon" in Winnemucca, Nevada. A lonely c. 1905 "Commercial" Trade Stimulator made by Mills Novelty Co. of Chicago sits at the end of the bar.

1940s: Night Scene in Reno Published by Nevada Photo Service of Reno. Center Street glowing with neon.

1940s: Postcard from Las Vegas A Realphoto of players at a busy roulette table in the Apache Casino of Las Vegas, Nevada.

1940s: Las Vegas Postcard It promotes the developing oasis in the desert.

1905: Postcard "Easy Street" from a painting by A. McC. Bell in 1904. Published by Blaesi & Bell. A skull in front of roulette layout and dice depicts the perils of trying to live on "Easy Street."

1905: Postcard "What's the Use?" from a painting by A. McC. Bell in 1904, published by Blaesi & Bell. With the skull wearing a pirate's hat in front of cards and dice, the artist appears to be saying that no matter how you play 'em, you'll still end up in the same place.

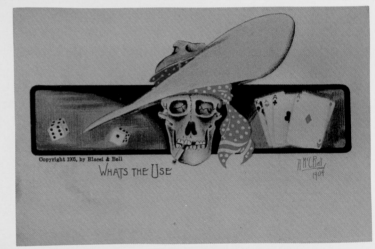

1913: Reynolds Postcard Reproduced from a Reynolds painting. Titled, "A Quiet Game," this is a somewhat idealized image of four cowboys playing poker against a backdrop of mountains and water.

1903: Monte Carlo Postcard This card is beautifully embossed with very realistic gold coins, as they are shown along with a deck topped by the Ace of Hearts. The Goddess Fortuna with her coin filled cornucopia embellishes the S of "Souvenir."

c. 1910: Monte Carlo Pig Postcard Embossed, with gold ink printing, it was published by Artist Ateliers H.Guggenheim & Co. of Zurich. Just like his horseshoe on the chain, the pig is a symbol of good luck in Europe. This is especially noticeable in cards and other objects from the Monte Carlo Casino in Monaco, where the pig is often shown as almost human, and always extremely prosperous.

1895: Monte Carlo Pig Postcard Marked, "Edition Guggenheim & Co., Zurich." The pig is considered to be a symbol of good luck all throughout Europe. Other good luck symbols shown on the card are a horseshoe, two four leaf clovers, a lady bug and a magic mushroom. The ball has landed in number 13 on the roulette wheel.

c. 1910: Monte Carlo Pig Postcard Generous gold ink in printing by Edition Guggenheim & Co., Zurich. This prosperous (un plein) pig appears to have gone hogwild and is attempting to devour the entire roulette wheel.

c. 1895: Monte Carlo Roulette Postcard Marked, "Artist. Ateliers H. Guggenheim & Co. Zurich." Embossed card showing a fashionably dressed woman in a carriage drawn by two donkeys, with a roulette wheel shown as the wheel of the carriage.

c. 1905: Monte Carlo Roulette Postcard Marked, "Edition Guggenheim & Co. Zurich." Out for an afternoon spin, this very early convertible in Monte Carlo rolls along on roulette wheel tires.

c. 1900: Monte Carlo Roulette Postcard Embossed, with gold ink printing by Edition Guggenheim & Co., Zurich. Note the stamp and Monte Carlo Casino cancellation in the lower right hand corner of this postcard depicting a lovely lady croupier framed by a roulette wheel.

c. 1910: Monte Carlo Pig Postcard Embossed, with gold ink printing, published by Artist Ateliers H. Guggenheim of Zurich. A glamorous young woman holding a 20 franc coin is riding on the lucky pig whose feet are standing on a roulette layout.

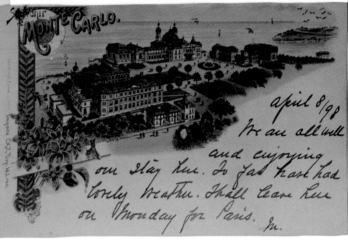

April 7, 1898: Monte Carlo Postcard Published by Charles Glogau of Nice, France. The drawings depict the room for the game of Trente et Quarante (Thirty and Forty), as well as the magnificent concert hall, and other buildings on the grounds of Monte Carlo.

April 8, 1898: Monte Carlo Postcard Published by Carl Kunzli of Zurich. Drawing of a panoramic view of the casino grounds and gardens. This card, as well as the Charles Glogau card, were both sent by the same person to a Miss Thompson in New York City.

c. 1900: Monte Carlo Roulette Postcard Printed by Louis Glaser of Leipsig. Salle de Roulette (Roulette Room) of Monte Carlo Casino. It shows a photo of the roulette room in the casino and a drawing of L'Heureux Gagnant (The Happy Winner) who has become the center of attention.

c. 1900: Monte Carlo Postcard Embossed painted scene of formally dressed donkeys, sheep and geese gambling in La Salle du Jeu (The Playing Room) of the elegant Monte Carlo Casino.

c. 1900: Monte Carlo Roulette Postcard Printed by Louis Glaser of Leipsig. Photo of Roulette Room in the casino, the men on either side are: "La Chance" (The Lucky One) and "La Guigne" (The Unlucky One).

1905: Ullman Postcards This is one of a set of postcards, printed by Ullman Mfg. Co. of New York, expanding creatively upon the imagery of court cards. The King of Diamonds is most aptly represented by a baseball player, who scores by running around the four bases of the baseball diamond.

1905: Ullman Postcards The Queen of Spades is adorned with spade jewelry as bracelets, necklace and pins on her dress, as well as what might be a spade bonnet on her head. Does holding a rose suggest that she's been digging in the garden?

1905: Ullman Postcards A turn of the century policeman holds his billy club to signify his role as King of Clubs.

1905: Ullman Postcards Is the inference on this Queen of Clubs that her monogram and medals suggest she belongs to some club--or that her majorette twirling pins are to be seen as clubs?

CAST YOUR BREAD UPON THE WATERS

The Johanna Smith was not only the "World's Most Famous Gambling Ship," but also the first to operate in international waters. Gambling ships existed between 1928 and 1946, with as many as 20 ships, although no more than four to six were operating at the same time. While the Johanna Smith made claim to being the most famous, the Rex and the Tango were to become far more popular a decade later. These floating casinos featured Black Jack, roulette, craps, slot machines, poker, pharo, and other casino games, along with sports betting. There were also dancing and fine restaurants.

These ships were operating in the waters along the coast of Southern California, beyond the three mile limit, outside the jurisdiction of federal or state law enforcement. They were protected from prosecution by the laws and the lawyers. Each ship was properly registered, having a licensed captain, and attempting to operate in a legal fashion in every manner.

When the Rex opened for business on May 5, 1938, it had 150 slot machines on board and 325 employees. There were full page advertisements for this opening in local newspapers, along with sky writing and radio advertising. The ads never mentioned gambling but used discreet statements such as "Thrills found only beyond the Three Mile Limit" and "Dining, dancing and a million thrills await you".

The Rex was visited by an average of 2,500 guests every 24 hours in its first year of operation, although the capacity was held to 1990 at any one time. Water taxi speedboats, which carried the customers to the gambling ships from the Long Beach and Santa Monica piers, cost 25 cents; the return trip was free. The ride could be as short as ten minutes.

Earl Warren, as California Attorney General in 1939, was determined to shut the ships down, but was unsuccessful for seven years. In 1946 as Governor of California, he succeeded in getting new federal and state legislation passed, and was finally able to sink the operation. Unfortunately, very little memorabilia from this chapter in gambling history has surfaced.

During World War II, many older gambling ships, including the Rex, served their country and became troop or cargo carriers.

1929 Johanna Smith Postcard

April, 1940: Crime Detective Magazine published by Crime Detective Inc. of Dunellen, New Jersey. Cover painting by Lewis Berg illustrates a short story titled "Gambling Ship Girl."

1940: Gambling on the High Seas This theatre lobby card from Warner Bros. shows a casino scene aboard a ship, complete with a roulette wheel on an ornately carved table, numbers wheel, slot machines and a baccarat table.

c. 1907: Bucking the Tiger A 26.5" x 40" Cyrus Noble Whiskey printed advertisement, using a painting based on a famous 1893 photograph of a pharo game at the Oriental Saloon in Tombstone/Bisbee, Arizona. The clothing of the players and spectators, as well as some of the decor in the saloon, have been changed to give a more stereotypical version of the late nineteenth century western saloon. This advertisement was also printed in a smaller size, 8.5" x 12.75", on cardboard.

c. 1910: The Double "O" Printed 26.5" x 40" advertisement for Cyrus Noble and W.A. Lacey Whiskies from Crown Distilleries of New York, San Francisco and Cincinnati, done by Clarence M. Leavy. This well known advertising print is based upon a roulette game and is often thought of as a companion piece to the Cyrus Noble pharo game ad. This image was also printed in a smaller size, 8.5" x 12.75", on cardboard.

Chapter Three:
HAVE I GOT A DEAL FOR YOU

Antique advertising has been one of the fastest growing areas in the entire spectrum of memorabilia collecting. During the 1980s rare and desirable advertising signs of this unique form of Americana routinely sold for many thousands of dollars. The record price for an advertising sign is $93,500, which was paid for a tin Campbell's Soup advertisement that resembled an American flag. (It was sold by Oliver's Auction house of Kennebunk, Maine in July of 1990.)

Advertisements with playing card and gambling imagery are among some of the most interesting antiques collectors can find today. They contained subtle hints suggesting that if you bought a particular product, you too could be a winner. To give the idea that some particular product was the best, it was shown alongside an unbeatable hand in a card game, or named "Trump" or "Ace". A picture of a game of cards, or one of well dressed people at a roulette wheel in an elegant casino, attempted to associate different types of products with times of pleasure and recreation.

Playing card and gambling images on the packaging of various products of the past were usually very colorful, sometimes serious, sometimes humorous. Today they can be found on tobacco tins, cigar boxes, liquor bottles, serving trays, cookie tins, automobile products, shaving materials, and many other familiar consumer items. Many of the messages, often for liquor or tobacco, were designed to appeal directly to gamblers and card players.

Gambling images and phrases appeared on billboards, on posters and signs in retail shops, restaurants and bars, and in newspaper and magazine ads. Some of the more common phrases sometimes shown alongside hands of cards or dice have been "Our best deal", "Blue chip quality", "You can't lose", "Be a winner", "Why gamble?", "Don't pass up this deal", or "Best deal in town".

In the past, when a particular gambling theme was popular and effective, many other manufacturers would copy it. The phrase and image of "Four Aces" was used repeatedly to connote the best, even after the 1870s when this hand was no longer the best hand in poker, having been replaced by a royal flush.

Another form of advertising collectibles are decks of playing cards with advertising printed on them. *(See Chapter Ten)*. The product being advertised often appeared on the backs of the cards, the ace of spades, the joker, and on the box. Advertising on playing cards began in the 1870s. It is thought that the first American deck of this kind was for Dr. Ransom's Medicine, c. 1870, and that it is the only advertising deck without corner indices. The heyday of playing card advertising was between 1890 and 1910, but this form of advertising is still being used effectively today.

Turn of the century clay chips incised with advertising messages are also of great interest. They were primarily ads for various alcoholic beverages or different brands of tobacco, especially cigars, but chips have also been used to advertise casinos, department stores, food products, automobiles, World's Fairs, or even the company that manufactured the chips.

The language and images of gambling appear in many ways in the messages of advertising, selling and packaging, and it is this fact that makes antique advertising of interest to the collector of gambling memorabilia.

1926: Double "OO" Cigar Tin Manufactured in Nevada, the image on this label was borrowed from a painting that was also used for a well-known Cyrus Noble whiskey ad. It shows a group of players at a game of roulette. The paper label attached to the 3.5" x 5.5" x 1.25" metallic green tin announces that the price for the cigars are 10 cents each.

c. 1910: Four Aces American Rye Whiskey Made by British Columbia Distillery Co. Ltd, of New Westminster, B.C., Canada. Although the Four Ace label is interesting, it is far surpassed by the heavy glass bottle itself. The bottle was cast into an overall bas relief pattern of Aces, using all four suit signs. This pattern covers the entire bottle except for the neck and the rectangular sections reserved for the labels, making this one of the most interesting bottles I've ever seen. The back label instructs the user to break the bottle when empty so that it would not be refilled with inferior contents. This might explain why I've never seen another one.

Four Aces! Left: 1920s cigarette lighter advertising "Four Aces American Rye Whiskey." The advertisement shows a spread of Four Aces on the pearlized celluloid that covers the body of the lighter, printed in translucent brown and red inks, the inks allowing the pearlescent material to shine through as the faces of the cards. Right: 1940s box of "specially tempered" razor blades made in England. On the outside of the box, again we see the hand of Four Aces, by inference "the best you can get." The wrappers on the blades inside show the four suit signs and repeat the brand name "Four Aces." It is interesting to note that these items were manufactured at least fifty years after Four Aces was no longer the best hand in poker.

c. 1910: Burger Brewing Beer Tray 12" x 15" oval metal tray made for the Burger Brewing Co. of Cincinnati. Depicts a bottle of their brand of beer and suggests its similarity to German brews by the dialect in the question, "Vas you efer in Zinzinnati?" Note the combination of the pipe, two glasses of beer and a deck of cards, suggesting a pleasant time.

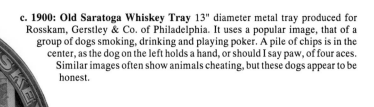

c. 1900: Old Saratoga Whiskey Tray 13" diameter metal tray produced for Rosskam, Gerstley & Co. of Philadelphia. It uses a popular image, that of a group of dogs smoking, drinking and playing poker. A pile of chips is in the center, as the dog on the left holds a hand, or should I say paw, of four aces. Similar images often show animals cheating, but these dogs appear to be honest.

c. 1900: Clay Advertising Chips Advertising the Lembeck & Betz Eagle Brewing Co. of Jersey City, New Jersey, each chip was incised with an eagle sitting on a rock showing the name of the company. Max Klein's chips from Allegheny, Pennsylvania show a bottle of Silver Age Rye on both sides. The backs have writing circling around the top of the chip, saying, "Drink Silver Age Rye."

Beer and Cigarettes Left: This 2.75" x 4.5" label for Royal Beer made by the Reno Brewing Company of Reno, Nevada depicts a hand holding a Royal Flush. The ad line is "It can't be beat." Right: Again we see the visual motif and the product name of Four Aces on these cigarettes made by W.D. & H.O. Wills Ltd. of Bristol and London in the 1920s.

c. 1910: Tip Tray From the Leisy Brewing Co. of Peoria, Illinois, this 5" diameter tin tray with enamel paint was manufactured by Kaufmann and Strauss in New York. These trays were usually placed on the tables or near the cash register in a saloon, this one obviously from an area where the card game of Skat was a popular one. The game of Skat is played with a deck of 32 cards.

1904: Teddy Roosevelt Political Button Manufactured by the Stand Pat Button Co. of Detroit, Michigan. 1.25" metal button with hand holding Four Aces marked with the four major points of Teddy Roosevelt's platform, "Prosperity, Protection, Expansion and Sound Money," along with Roosevelt himself as the fifth card. Using the poker term "Stand Pat" which means "I'll keep my hand as it is," the button is telling voters to keep Roosevelt for another term. He had been Vice President under McKinley and became President upon the assassination of McKinley in 1901.

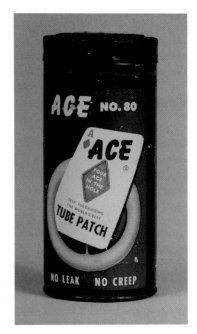

Late 1930s: Ace Tube Patch Cement This cylindrical 4.5" high can of material to patch the inner tubes of tires was made by Ace Rubber Co. of Dallas, Texas. It uses an Ace to suggest the best, and the phrase, "Your Ace in the Hole," as a pun on the hole in the tube and a reference to the closed card in Five Card Stud Poker, a game that was very popular at that time.

c. 1940: Nasher Post Card Advertising Nasher Clothes of Stoughton, Massachusetts, this card was printed in Teknitone Process by E.B. Thomas of Cambridge, Massachusetts. It makes use of a Royal Flush, and the playing card phrase "A New Deal." The use of the phrase "New Deal," so popularized by the social programs of President Franklin Delano Roosevelt in the thirties, is a good example of how terms that originate with card playing become a part of everyday language.

Two Tobacco Products The 2.5" x 3.75" package on the left is a muslin bag of rolling tobacco from Wm. S. Kimball & Co./American Tobacco Co. of Maryland, c. 1895. The name "Pedro," along with the Jack of Spades in the design, are probably a reference to the card game of Pedro Sancho, popular in the late nineteenth century. The 3" round tin on the right, was made in England for Cope Bros. & Co. Ltd. of Liverpool and London, in the 1920s. It uses the popular design of Four Aces, as well as the brand name "High Card," to suggest the high quality of their chewing tobacco.

c. 1890: Clay Advertising Chips The chips on the top row say, "Chew Lorillard's SPLENDID Plug Tobacco." The bottom row advertises, "M. Stachelberg & Co's. Cigars," with a cigar incised in the center.

Five Tobacco Tins from the turn of the century. Courtesy of *Past Times,* a newsletter for collectors of antique advertising. (See Contacts List)

No. 5457 ins
No. 5458 outs
Price for Set: 2 cts. net.

Straight Five Cigars Salesman's sample label for a cigar box. Depicts a hand holding a Straight Flush of Ace to five of Hearts. The image and name refer to the fact that the cigar cost five cents.

c. 1890: Five Cent Ante Advertising Poster 7" x 11" cardboard sign from P. Lorillard & Co. advertising Five Cent Ante Chewing Tobacco. It shows a poker hand of four Aces, poker chips and a border of suit signs, targeting the ad for poker players.

c. 1930: Pimm's Tin Advertising Plate This 10" diameter plate has a border of five sets of playing card suit signs. The center depicts a mug of Pimm's Number One Iced Tea sitting on an Ace of Hearts, surrounded by the words "Pimm's No.1 Cup."

c. 1890: The New Bachelor Cigar Tin This 5" high rectangular tin with rounded corners that held 25 cigars makes use of the image of a man playing a game of solitaire, while dreaming about a woman and smoking New Bachelor cigars. It also shows the cigar box of the same brand.

1930s: Trump Cookies Tin Canister This 5.75" high tin manufactured by the Pacific Coast Biscuit Co. held one pound of butter wafer cookies in the shapes of the four suit signs. Despite the wording printed on the back of the tin suggesting that these cookies were "especially suited for serving at bridge teas," along with the bridge term "trump" as the name of the product, the manufacturer chose to depict the best hand in poker--a Royal Flush.

c. 1920s: Sandy Tricks Cookie Tin Manufactured for J.S. Ivins' Son, Inc. of Philadelphia, Pennsylvania, this 5.5" high tin contained small butter cookies in the shapes of the four playing card suit signs. The design on the printed canister shows four Aces circling the can, a magician between the Ace of Clubs and Ace of Diamonds doing card tricks, and various groupings of people playing cards around the sides.

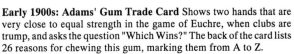

1883: A & P Trade Card Printed for the Atlantic and Pacific Tea Company, that we know today as the A & P Supermarket chain, to promote their tea and coffee over a century ago. A poker game between a dog and a monkey, both humanized enough to drink liquor from glasses and smoke cigars. The monkey has a red Ace tucked under his right arm while his tail curls around another Ace. Numerous images of monkeys cheating may have led to the common poker expression, "Don't monkey with the cards."

1913: Mennen's Shaving Cream Back page advertisement from a 10" x 14" *Harper's* magazine shows four Kings and four Jacks, their faces covered from the nose down, and asks if the reader can remember which card figures have beards or mustaches. The ad assures that Mennen's is the best shaving preparation for any kind of beard. This is typical of the advertising use of gambling and card playing images that were so often directed toward men.

1888: Lottery Advertising Card Trade card advertising "The Original Little Louisiana Co." from Kansas City, Missouri. First Prize $7,500 for 50 cent ticket; $3,750 for 25 cent ticket. The reverse side claims, "We are the original. All others are imitations." and "Prizes paid in full in U.S. gold coin at Kansas City, Missouri."

1949: "Night Unto Night" Starring Ronald Reagan Theatre Lobby Card from Warner Bros. Pictures Corporation. The young President-to-be looks worried as he plays cards with two actresses. Mr. President, were you bluffing?

1951: "Night into Morning" Produced by Metro-Goldwyn-Mayer. The young actress in the center is the woman we now know as Nancy Reagan! AN AMAZING COINCIDENCE! While this film made in 1951 was titled "Night into Morning," just two years earlier the film on the theatre lobby card showing Ronald Reagan playing cards was titled "Night unto Night."

Chapter Four:
AND THE ACADEMY AWARD GOES TO...

Perhaps more than any other source, Hollywood has shaped both our perceptions and fantasies about gambling and gamblers. The cinema has left us with a huge array of treasured images of many of our favorite movie stars playing cards or flirting with Lady Luck in various gambling scenes. Most of the memorabilia is confined to theater lobby cards, 11" x 14", or lobby publicity photos, 8" x 10", which were distributed nationally by film companies to promote their films.

The search for theater lobby cards with famous actors and actresses, playing pharo in a western frontier saloon, or at a friendly game of poker, or standing at a roulette wheel in an elegant casino, is a rewarding experience. With a small investment of time, effort, energy and money, you can locate large dealers of Hollywood memorabilia all across the country who will be happy to help you find what you are looking for. Many of these dealers have accumulated thousands of lobby cards and lobby photos and the cost is usually quite low. In addition, there are frequent Hollywood/movie memorabilia shows in most large cities where valuable contacts can be established. In publications about antiques and collectibles there are names of people and organizations who will lead you in the right direction.

Lobby cards are fun to collect and I often find myself looking through these items of nostalgia in my own collection. I have sold my duplicates to friends who frame them and often for less than a total cost of $25 have a conversation piece hanging on the wall. My own favorite films about gambling are "House of Games," "Guys and Dolls," "Showboat," "Funny Girl," "The Hustler," "A Big Hand for the Little Lady," "The Sting," "Oceans Eleven," "The Gamblers," "California Split," "The Cincinnati Kid," "Five Against the House," "The Lady Eve," and "Mr. Lucky." I continually search for particular heroes of my youth and have included many of them in this chapter. A vast number of Hollywood's gambling scenes with famous movie stars await your search.

1945: "Adventure" Starring Clark Gable and Greer Garson Theatre Lobby Card from Metro Goldwyn Mayer. The young couple have a twinkle in their eyes after receiving their chips from a winning bet at roulette. Is it love or is it money when Clark exclaims, "I've been lucky since the day I met you, baby"?

1949: "**Any Number Can Play**" A Loews' Theatre lobby photo of a film by Metro-Goldwyn-Mayer shows Clark Gable having a serious discussion with several other well known actors at a poker table in a casino. Note Chuck-a-Luck cage behind them.

1966: "**Frankie and Johnny**" with "The King," Elvis Presley, as Johnny. United Artists Corp. This scene shows Elvis playing Draw Poker in a saloon and requesting two cards. However, he is not playing his cards "close to the vest," making the mistake of revealing his cards to the woman behind him, as well as to the bartender. If he continues to flash his cards in this manner he will soon become "All Shook Up."

1957: "**The Joker is Wild**" **Starring Frank Sinatra, Mitzi Gaynor, Eddie Albert and Jeanne Crain** Theatre Lobby Card from Paramount Pictures Corp. "The Chairman of the Board" seems casual and relaxed as he enjoys a poker game at home.

1957: "**Loving You" Starring Elvis Presley** Theatre lobby color photo by Paramount Pictures. A friendly poker game in a small hotel lobby is interrupted while Elvis stands by watching.

c. 1948: "**Lucky Losers" with Leo Gorcey, Huntz Hall and The Bowery Boys** Monogram Pictures. Note how the four suit signs are used as the theme for the design of the card.

c. 1948: "**Lucky Losers**" Some of the Bowery Boys running the craps table at a fancy casino, perhaps having learned from their experiences "out on the street." Note the "unusual" situation of two sets of dice on the table at the same time.

c. 1938: Bud Abbott & Lou Costello Publicity photo showing the famous comedy team of Abbott and Costello shooting dice in a bathroom on a train.

1944: "Three of a Kind" An 8" x 10" publicity photo using the imagery of three aces, each showing a well-known actor. Shemp Howard, one of the Three Stooges, is the Ace of Hearts. The Ace of Diamonds is Slapsie Maxie Rosenbloom, a well-known champion boxer and Hollywood actor. The Ace of Spades is actor Billy Gilbert.

c. 1940: "Gangs of New York" Starring Charles Bickford Produced by Republic Pictures. The numbers on the roulette layout serve as a desk for the gang's attempts to balance the numbers in their books.

1934: "'Now I'll Tell' by Mrs. Arnold Rothstein" Starring Spencer Tracy and Alice Faye In this theatre lobby photo, Tracy sits at the poker table with a large pot of chips still in the center. Carolyn Greene was the wife of Arnold Rothstein, who is most remembered for allegedly arranging the outcome of the World Series of 1919. However, Rothstein was never convicted for that crime or for any other crimes.

1941: "The Blonde From Singapore" Starring Leif Erikson Produced by Columbia Pictures Corp. A dispute seems to be brewing at the roulette table in an elegant club.

1956: "Johnny O'Clock" Starring Dick Powell and Evelyn Keyes Produced by Columbia Pictures Corp. Proprietor Dick Powell sits at his desk in the center of this casino scene where the dealers and ropes separate him from the players of Roulette, Black Jack, Craps and Hazard. There is a clear shot of a Hazard layout at the lower left.

1949: "The Undercover Man" Starring Glenn Ford Produced by Columbia Pictures Corp. Scene of a crowded casino with Black Jack, Craps and a Five Stud Poker game. Five Stud Poker was one of the most popular forms of poker from the 1920s to the 1950s.

1937: "North of the Rio Grande" Starring William Boyd (Hopalong Cassidy) and Russell Hayden In this theatre lobby photo from Paramount Pictures, George "Gabby" Hayes is seated at the piano as Hoppy appears to have his mind more on the Black Jack dealer than the Black Jack deal.

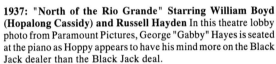

1940: "The Showdown" Starring William Boyd (Hopalong Cassidy) and Russell Hayden Lobby photo from Paramount Pictures. Hopalong, seated at the right with his gun on the table, is at a Draw Poker game in which the bow-tied dealer is carelessly or purposely revealing the top two cards he is about to deal, which appear to be of great interest to the player at the left.

c. 1940: "Bordertown Gun Fighters" Starring George "Gabby" Hayes Produced by Republic Pictures. Gabby co-starred with more Western stars than nearly any other actor. In this scene, he is about to place a bet on the roulette table.

1948: "Loaded Pistols" Starring Gene Autry, Barbara Britton and the Wonder Horse, Champion Gene Autry shows that he could be more than the "Singing Cowboy" by putting a quick halt to a crooked craps game which even included the marshall.

c. 1948: "The Carson City Kid" Starring Roy Rogers, King of the Cowboys Republic Pictures. A fight is about to erupt in the poker game as the player with four aces is reaching for the pot, and the player with four kings has a problem with how they managed to obtain those hands.

c. 1935: "Land of the Outlaws" Starring Johnny Mack Brown Produced by Monogram Pictures. In this scene, Brown is a Black Jack dealer who has spotted something irregular and has grabbed the wrist of the cowboy dressed in black. This actor is Charles "Blackie" King, one of the "great" villains of the Sagebrush Cinema.

c. 1935: "Flashing Guns" Starring Johnny Mack Brown Produced by Monogram Pictures. Brown confidently shows his cards at a Draw Poker game, and is about to take the money from the pot as the players at the roulette table in the rear of the gambling hall stop to watch.

c. 1940: "Sierra Passage" Produced by Monogram Pictures. A familiar Hollywood scene in which the good guy (white hat and clean shaven) aims his cocked guns at the scoundrels (black hats and unshaven). The chips still lying in the pot at the center of the table reveal that the poker game has been interrupted quite suddenly.

1946: "The Renegades" Produced by Columbia Pictures Corp. Early Western saloon shootout scene with a 1900 "Chicago" floor model slot machine made by Mills Novelty Co., and a Chuck-a-Luck cage and layout on the table near the swinging doors. A Pharo table is at the far left wall.

c. 1930: "Shotgun Pass" Starring Tim McCoy Two "dance hall women" look down from the balcony as Col. Tim McCoy, center, stands near a well-worn roulette table. McCoy was one of the most popular western stars of the period. He was born in 1891 and died in 1978, serving in World War I and gaining the rank of Lieutenant Colonel.

1940: "Wells Fargo Gunmaster" Starring Allan "Rocky" Lane and his stallion Black Jack Produced by Republic Pictures. Rocky Lane (left) is at the roulette table in a western gambling hall.

1951: "Trail Guide" Starring Tim Holt Produced by RKO Radio Pictures Inc. Holt (in red shirt) stands by a roulette table, handing a gun to the man on his left. In 1948 Tim Holt was nominated for an Oscar as best supporting actor for his role in "The Treasure of Sierra Madre" which starred Humphrey Bogart.

1868: How Gamblers Win or the Secrets of Advantage Playing by "A Retired Professional." A 4" x 6.5" soft cover paperback with 112 pages. It was published by Fitzgerald Publishing Corporation who claimed to be the successor to Dick & Fitzgerald, but the latter company was still publishing many years later. The devilish character on the cover is clearly meant to represent those who cheated, or more politely put, those who used "advantage" playing. The first page explains the book as, "Being a complete and scientific expose of the manner of playing all the various advantages as practiced by professional gamblers upon the uninitiated."

Chapter Five:
NEVER GAMBLE WITH STRANGERS

By the mid-1860s there were three companies manufacturing gambling equipment. Will & Finck began its long career in San Francisco in 1863; Mason & Co. began as Mason & Metzger in Chicago in 1867; and, on the east coast, in New York City, E.M. Grandin started in 1864. These companies manufactured both regular and "special," "controlled," or "advantage playing" gambling equipment. "Special," "controlled," and "advantage playing" were the euphemistic terms used to denote apparatus that could be used for cheating. Such items are often referred to as "gaffed."

Between those times and 1961, there have been hundreds, perhaps thousands, of companies that have manufactured and sold devices for cheating purposes. Large gambling supply manufacturers also outfitted carnivals with a huge variety of games and equipment, most of which were not what they appeared to be. In 1935, in Chicago alone, there were over 50 gambling supply factories that produced various types of cheating equipment. In the almost century long history of many gambling supply companies, they had sold just about every conceivable product that could be used to swindle, defraud and separate innocent victims from their money.

In 1961, new legislation gave the Interstate Commerce Commission the legal power to prevent interstate transportation of almost all items that might be used as cheating devices, thus a dark chapter in the history of gambling was brought to a close. These cheating devices have now become artifacts of history, desirable only as antique collectibles from a bygone era.

Many books written between 1843 and 1961 exposed and explained methods of cheating, often as warnings to innocent players about "Sharpers" or "Sharps," those who used crooked methods in gambling. The authors discussed such things as confidence games, loaded dice, reflective mirrors, magnetic devices, and many other types of "advantage playing." Numerous books were written about card manipulation. Card manipulators were referred to as "Mechanics." The authors warned players by discussing and illustrating false cuts, false shuffles, switching cards, crimping cards, arranging (stacking) cards, second or bottom dealing, using marked or altered cards, applying colorless wax "Daub," introducing a "Cold Deck," and other dishonest moves and methods.

Quite a few of these books were written by people who were reformed gamblers, such as Jonathan Harrington Green, who wrote *An Exposure of the Arts and Miseries of Gambling* in 1843, the first known book of this type. Some other reformed gamblers who wrote about cheating were Kid Royal, John Philip Quinn, Mason Long, and Kid Canfield, not to be confused with Richard Canfield (1855-1914) owner of casinos in Saratoga and New York City.

Some of the most interesting cheating devices, from a collector's point of view, are the hold-out machines. These devices allowed a crooked gambler to make a card or even an entire deck suddenly appear, as if it had been there all along. This was done by attaching these various hold-out devices to the ankles, arms or chest, as shown in the illustrations. Very few hold-outs have survived through the years and

1907: "Monkey Business" Postcard published by Julius Bien & Co. of New York, titled "A Skin Game" which means being fleeced right down to your bare skin. The Ace of Spades is being passed between the two well-dressed monkeys, while the center one looks on, naked and perplexed.

they are greatly valued by those collectors who use them as interesting displays along with pharo equipment, playing cards and Early Western memorabilia.

One oft told tale was about the inventor of a hold-out device, a man named Kepplinger. After a suspiciously long series of wins at poker games in 1888, Kepplinger was discovered to be cheating - but the game happened to include many other cheaters. When they stripped him to see if he was wearing a hold out device, they found a strange new instrument that consisted of wires, wheels, joints, tubes, string, and pulleys. Instead of punishing him, they promised not to divulge his secret on one condition. They insisted that he make identical devices for each of them! They never played together again. Today, most collectors refer to any large hold out as a "Kepplinger."

Perhaps more than any other cheating systems, marked cards and "prepared cards" were the most commonly used by the criminal player. These cards were referred to as "Readers". Almost every gambling supply company that issued catalogs, provided their customers with cards marked or altered by a myriad of methods. These companies would purchase the most common brands of decks manufactured by large playing card companies and would mark or alter the cards. They would then repackage the decks as if they had never been opened. Various types of "prepared cards" were referred to as humps, strippers, bellies, trimmed, sanded, waxed, slick, rounded corners, and others. All of these were altered by the slightest adjustments that were virtually undetectable to the unsuspecting eye. This enabled the devious player who was using these decks to locate and arrange certain cards. These types of items are of great interest to many of today's collectors.

Gambling supply catalogs are fascinating as items of gambling memorabilia. They provide a most valuable source of information on this subject and offer rare insights into the devious methods that were all too readily available prior to 1961. Some of the other favorites of those who collect cheating devices are the gaffed pharo dealing boxes *(See Chapter Six),* loaded dice, fixed carnival wheels, roulette tables with magnetic devices, "corner rounder" and "trimmer" tools to alter playing cards, and, of course, the antique books and magazines that are in any way related to cheating.

"EASY MONEY - How it's Made, How it's Lost" There were four issues of this 8.5" x 12" soft cover pulp magazine, each 96 pages, published in 1936 by the Spartan Publishing Corporation, Lexington Avenue, New York City. It was aimed at "young men: the boys who are tempted to make *Easy Money* the illegitimate way." It goes on to explain that "It is written to warn them that while *Easy Money* can be made, it cannot be obtained and enjoyed for long through the channels of crime...and to demonstrate that the straight road is the only safe route to *Easy Money.*" They promise to show the reader how some people have legitimately made fortunes in "swift, spectacular fashions." Also to show how others are trying to make "easy money" at the reader's expense. Twenty-five cents per issue, five issues for one dollar.

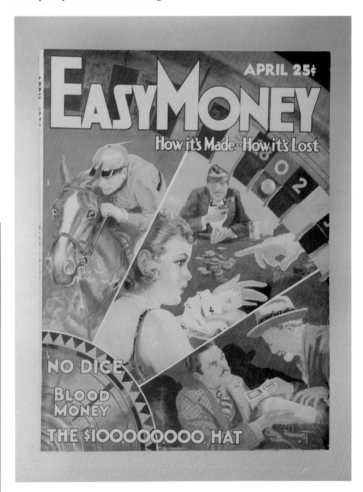

Above:
April, 1936: Volume One, Number One Cover design is from a painting by H.V.L. Parkhurst. The 14 stories include a Wall Street telephone boiler room operation, handicapping horses, craps with fixed or "murder" dice, tricking Lloyd's of London, and a Clergyman Swindler. There are also suggestions for how to start on the "road to your first million" by honest means.

Left:
May, 1936: Volume One, Number Two Cover design is from a painting by Charles McCann. The 16 stories include gaming percentages, cheaters who use marked cards, counterfeit money otherwise known as "queer money," and pitchmen and confidence games. Among suggestions for honest money making ideas are buying up old newspapers and then selling them as back issues, or setting up a service offering home grooming for pets.

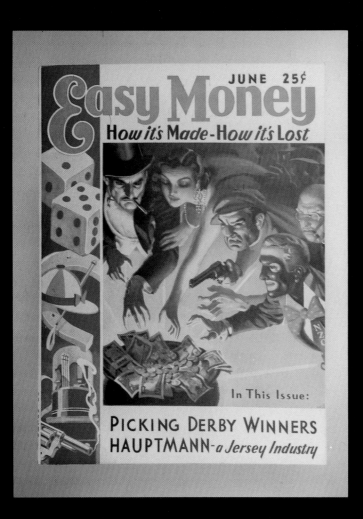

June, 1936: Volume One, Number Three Cover design from a painting by H.J. Ward. The 16 stories include choosing Kentucky Derby winners, how the average gambler is negatively affected by the house cut, and pin ball machines. The editors counsel that, "There is no Santa Claus, who in the guise of a perfect stranger, comes to you with a rare chance to pick up some easy money."

July, 1936: Volume One, Number Four Cover design from another painting by H.J. Ward. The 17 stories include how to handicap horse racing, the bookie's edge, an explanation of why bookmakers rarely lose, and baseball pools. It seems that the editors were running out of material, since this issue offered a prize of $1000 to the best letter about "The easiest money I ever made" or "How I was gypped," and no further issues seem to have been printed, despite an ad for the August issue.

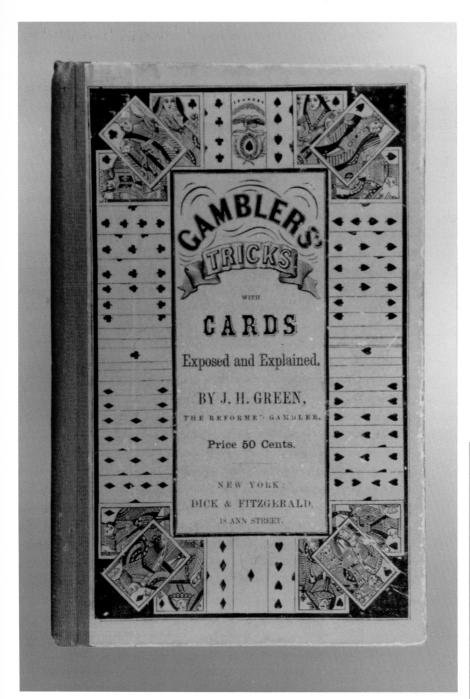

1859: Gamblers' Tricks With Cards Exposed and Explained by Jonathan Harrington Green, who referred to himself as "The Reformed Gambler." Published by Dick & Fitzgerald of New York, this is a 4.5" x 7" hard cover book with 114 pages. The cover shows 52 cards printed around the title on a deep yellow paper label attached to rust colored linen. Green was the first published author in America to have written books about gambling and to expose methods of cheating. With a great body of knowledge, he wrote and lectured extensively to warn inexperienced players against these methods.

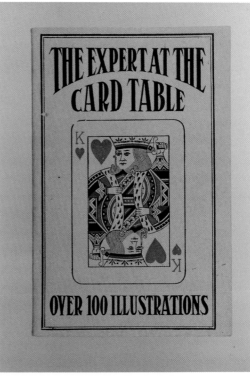

1902: The Expert at the Card Table by S.W. Erdnase (A reverse of E.S. Andrews, the author's real name) Published by Frederick J. Drake & Co. of Chicago, this is a 178 page, 4.25" x 6.5" soft paper cover book. It is illustrated with over 100 diagrams by M.D. Smith. The title page explains that the book is about, "artifice, ruse, and subterfuge at the card table. A treatise on the science and art of manipulating cards." This book was also published by K.C. Card Co. of Chicago in 1902, and then later published by Drake as a hardback edition in 1905.

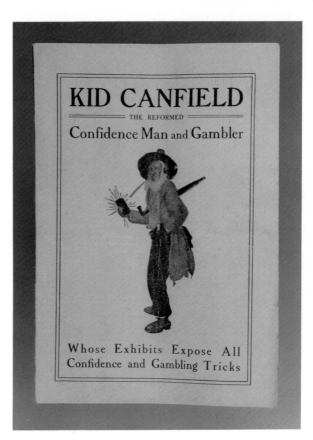

c. 1910: Card Sharpers by "Famous Reformed Confidence Man and Gambler," probably Kid Canfield. A 102 page, 5.25" x 7.75" soft paper cover book, the major portion of it is devoted to sleight-of-hand and card manipulation. Cheaters who used these particular methods were referred to as "Mechanics."

1911: Kid Canfield by George W. (Kid) Canfield. A 48 page, soft cover, 5.5" x 7.5" book, printed by Isaac Goldmann Co. of New York. "Gambling and confidence games exposed" appears on the title page. Canfield was born near Columbus, Ohio in 1878 and by 1899, he had opened two gambling houses in Coney Island, Brooklyn, N.Y. By 1911 he called himself "a reformed gambler," as Jonathan Harrington Green had done almost 70 years earlier.

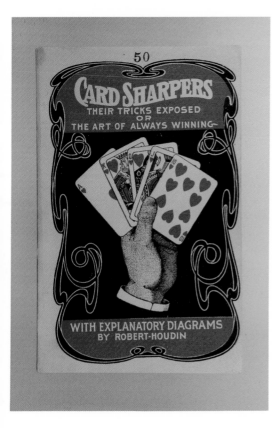

1902: Card Sharpers: Their Tricks Exposed or the Art of Always Winning A 4.5" x 7" soft cover paperback of 189 pages that was translated from the French of Robert Houdin by Wm. J. Hilliar. Published by Charles T. Powner of Chicago. This book was also published by Frederick J. Drake & Co. of Chicago, with a green cover showing the same hand with a Royal Flush. A man named Ehrich Weiss was so impressed with the knowledge, as well as the magical and mystical abilities of Mr. Houdin that he changed his name to *Harry Houdini*!

c. 1890: How Gamblers Cheat and The Treasure Casket of Mysteries Author unknown. Diamond Publishing Co. of Palmyra, Pennsylvania. The cover advertises that this 5" x 7" book of 100 pages includes, "Giving the methods employed by gamblers and revealing many secrets which were thought forever lost."

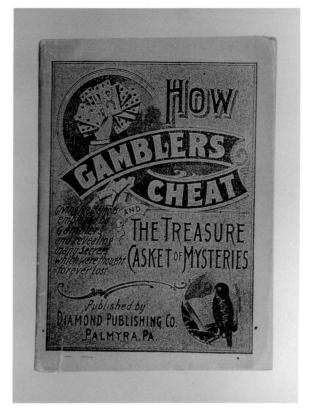

c. 1910: Wooldridge's Gambling Exposed A 32 page, 5" x 7.5" soft paper cover booklet, published by Max Stein Publishing House of Chicago. Called America's Sherlock Holmes on the cover, Clifton R. Wooldridge wrote about card hold-out devices, magnets to affect loaded dice, and "bucket shops," small businesses which were the site of some fraudulent transactions related to futures and options on the commodities market.

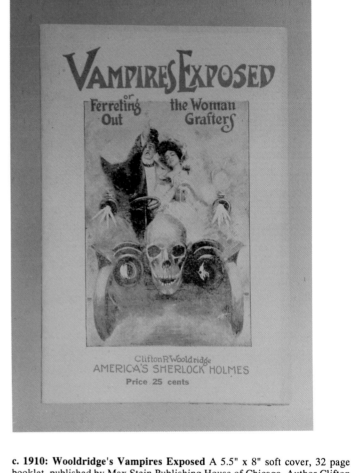

c. 1910: Wooldridge's Vampires Exposed A 5.5" x 8" soft cover, 32 page booklet, published by Max Stein Publishing House of Chicago. Author Clifton Wooldridge was a detective on the Chicago Police Force for 20 years. Wooldridge described cheaters and swindlers as vampires sucking the life blood of their victims.

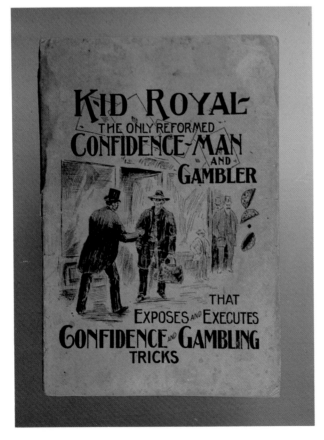

1896: Kid Royal The name of the author of this 5" x 7.5" book of 60 pages is given as H.W. Royal, the same name as the publishing company. Royal describes how both the proprietors of gambling houses and the players can be cheated in games of pharo, poker and roulette. He also exposes the most popular con games of the period, such as those used in Three Card Monte, Three Shell Game, Short Change and the Goldbrick Scheme. Despite the over 100 years of exposing Three Card Monte as a con game, and a game that cannot be beat, it is still widely "played" even today, especially in large cities and carnivals.

1911: Easy Money: or Fishing for Suckers by Harry Brolaski. Published by Searchlight Press of Cleveland, Ohio. Red and black ink printed on the 5.5" x 8" yellow linen hardcover. The title page of this 328 page book explains that the author is a "reformed gambler" and that the contents of the book are "All Gambling Tricks Exposed." Note the Devil's barbed fishing line attached to the large coin which holds the money that the people are about to greedily grasp.

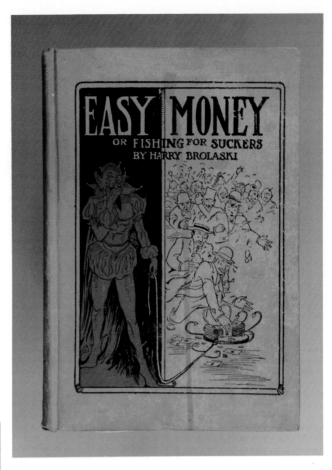

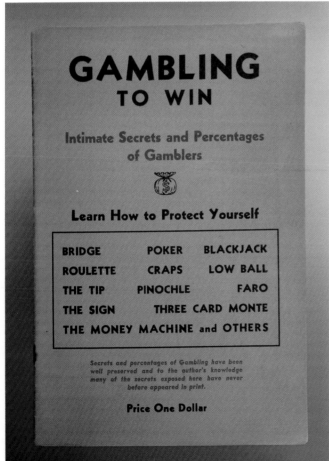

c. 1925: Gambling to Win A 24 page, heavy paper cover, 6" x 9" booklet, it reveals rackets and swindles in horse racing, Three Card Monte, card manipulation and dice switching.

1937: The High Art of Gambling A 94 page, 4.5" x 6" paperback book by Sir Anthony (A. Vitez Keresztfalvy) published by Monte Carlo Publishing Co. He describes "favorite winning systems" of successful gamblers in roulette, cards and dice. The first page starts out with the statement, "Do not gamble! This is the best advice I can give you." But the author then goes on to tell "how to win" if the reader insists upon gambling.

1930: A True Expose of Racketeers and Their Methods by Emmett Gowen. Published by Popular Book Corp of New York, it is an 8.5" x 12" soft cover book with 96 pages. Explains 40 different methods of cheating and swindles and is profusely illustrated with photos, such as of sidewalk hustlers, alongside the suggestions of how to spot them. The title page announces, "Tricks and treachery are the practice of fools that have not the wit to be honest," while the preface begins with the quote of the Apostle Paul from Timothy I, "The love of money is the root of all evil."

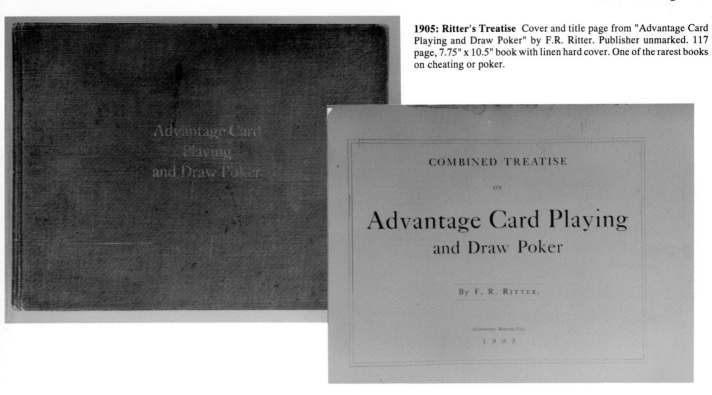

1905: Ritter's Treatise Cover and title page from "Advantage Card Playing and Draw Poker" by F.R. Ritter. Publisher unmarked. 117 page, 7.75" x 10.5" book with linen hard cover. One of the rarest books on cheating or poker.

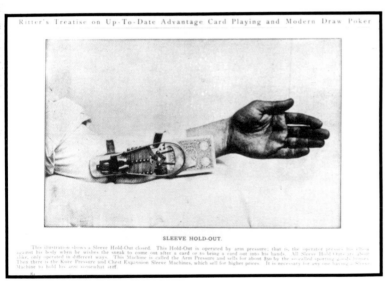

1905: Ritter's Treatise on Up-to-Date Advantage Card Playing and Draw Poker, page 84, showing a sleeve "Hold Out" cheating device. This photo shows the device before it has been extended, holding the card the player intends to deviously add to his hand by pressing the inside of his elbow against his body.

This second photo shows how the card slips directly into the hand. Using the term "advantage playing" for cheating seems a rather polite understatement.

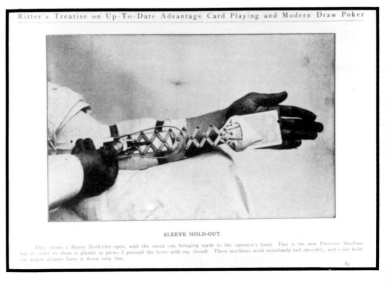

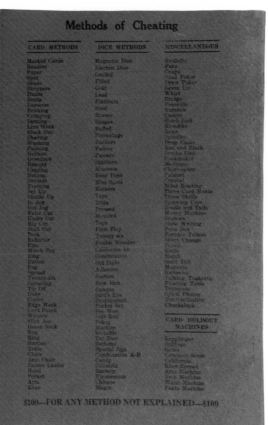

Left:
1925: Don't be a Sucker--Cheating Exposed Red and black, 5.75" x 8.75" soft cover book of 96 pages contains warnings against how cheating devices and deceptive methods are used.

Right:
1925: Don't be a Sucker--Cheating Exposed Back cover which offers a $100 reward for any cheating method not explained in the book.

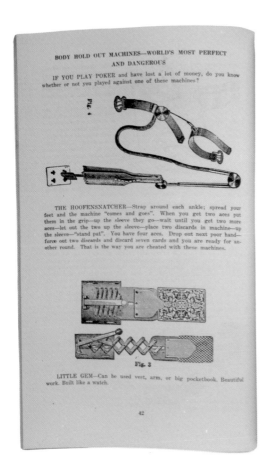

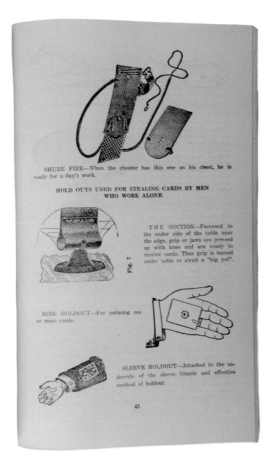

1925: Don't Be a Sucker--Cheating Exposed, pages 42 and 43. These pages show devices that allowed a crooked gambler to suddenly make a card, or even a whole new deck, appear by attaching the various devices to the ankles, arm or chest, or by using a clamp hidden under the table. The cheating methods described in the rest of the book include those used in poker and craps tables, magnetic dice, gaffed wheels, daub, marked cards and approximately 170 other schemes of cheating listed on the back page, either by a player or by a casino.

Left:
1929: Evans Catalog Cover of catalog from H.C. Evans & Co. in Chicago, using the brand name Evansmade. These 160 pages included many items for cheating.

Below left:
1929: Evans Catalog page 46. H.C. Evans & Co. of Chicago boldly advertised six card hold out devices, all shown in the photograph. They boasted, "Every hold out we list is made complete in our factory." Four are described below the photograph.

Below right:
1929: Evans Catalog page 48. Another catalog photograph of the hold out devices they manufactured and sold. The four devices in the photo are described on the page.

H.C. Evans & Co. ◆EVANSMADE◆ Chicago. Ill.

Card Holdout Machines

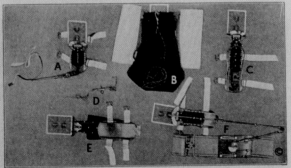

Every Holdout we list is made complete in our factory and although other firms advertise machines with similar or like names they are not the same and will not be as perfect in performance. We have a machine shop completely equipped to turn out the best and most accurate work it is possible to produce and our holdout machines are of the latest and most improved type. Another very important feature in connection with these machines is that when a customer finds a machine is not fitted to his use we will arrange a very liberal allowance toward the purchase of any other holdout machine desired.

Arm Pressure Holdout

This machine, style C above, is a favorite for the beginner as it is the most simple in construction of any machine made and is very easy to operate. It is of the Sullivan type, made of aluminum and steel and is very light and easy to handle. It is fitted with adjustable straps for fastening to the forearm and is operated by pressing the arm against the body. The receiver works on a Jacob's ladder and there is nothing to get out of order.
No. 20E284. Arm Pressure Holdout with instructions....................Each $25.00

California Holdout

This machine, style E above, is entirely different from the Sullivan machines and is operated with the hand flat on the table. It is made of aluminum and steel, simple in construction and one that can be operated with very little practice. The receiver is attached to a Jacob's ladder which operates the hook.
No. 20E287. California Holdout with instructions.....................Each $30.00

Common Sense Holdout

The Common Sense Holdout, style A above, is one of the most simple machines we manufacture and is particularly good for Draw. There are no strings or rubber bands and operation is smooth. The receiver is brought out by raising the arm which operates the Jacob's ladder. A small lever releases the catch allowing free arm movement independent of the machine. A good holdout for the beginner or the man of experience.
No. 20E289. Common Sense Holdout with instructions.....................Each $55.00

The Improved Cooler

This machine, style B above, is made to handle an entire deck, operating from the pants band. It is a thoroughly practical machine and one that gives complete satisfaction. The operation is simple and noiseless only one motion being necessary to bring up the deck and take care of the dead. This machine will fit any size man and we recommend that in ordering a pair of loose fitting trousers be sent us so we can have the machine fitted to them by our experienced tailors. There is no extra charge for this.
No. 20E295. Improved Cooler with instructions.....................Each $125.00

H.C. Evans & Co. ◆EVANSMADE◆ Chicago. Ill.

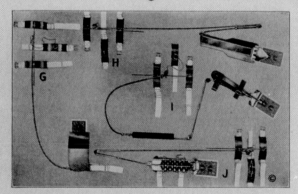

Gates Holdout

This machine, style I in the illustration, is the last word in a holdout machine and we cannot recommend it too highly for the practical machine operator. It is constructed on an entirely new principle of the best materials obtainable and is supplied to operate with either knee spread or straight leg movement, the knee spread being generally the most practical. A very small movement is sufficient to extend the receiver the full length and it comes and goes with the hand flat on the table. There is no ladder on this machine. The Gates Holdout is not a machine for the beginner but for the man who has had experience with tools of this kind it cannot be excelled. Particularly good for Black Jack or Stud.
No. 20E290. Gates Holdout with instructions.....................Each $125.00

Sullivan Holdouts

The Sullivan Holdout is supplied in two styles, both simple in construction and easy to operate. The Sullivan Knee Spread, style J in the illustration, operates with a knee spread movement. The Sullivan Chest Expansion, style F, requires a special belt with expansion plates. A very small movement is ample to extend the receiver the full length and either machine is very good for Draw.
No. 20E285. Sullivan Knee Spread Holdout with instructions.............Each $40.00
No. 20E286. Sullivan Chest Expansion Holdout with instructions.........Each 50.00

Keplinger Sleeve Holdout

This machine, style H in the illustration, is one of the most practical machines made and has met with great favor as it can be played with a soft flannel shirt. It is noiseless, no complicated parts and nothing to get out of order. The receiver operates on a slide and operates with knee spread or straight leg motion as preferred the knee spread being the most satisfactory. This is a good all around machine for the practical man.
No. 20E288. Keplinger Sleeve Holdout with instructions.....................Each $55.00

Vest Holdout

This machine, style G in the illustration, is not a sleeve machine but operates from the opening of the vest. It is simple and trouble proof and operates with a leg movement. The receiver is attached to a slide and we suggest the knee spread as being the most practical.
No. 20E293. Vest Holdout with instructions.....................Each $30.00

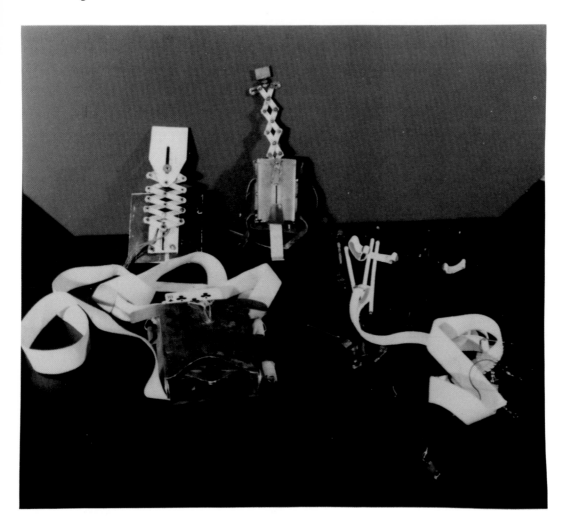

1920s: Hold Out Cheating Devices These hold out mechanisms which were made to be worn by the cheater beneath his clothing, were specifically manufactured for cheating at cards. Three of them used expandable "Jacob's Ladder" units that held cards and could be collapsed or extended by various methods. The one at the left forefront was made to hold an entire deck, which was known as "bringing or ringing in a Cold Deck."

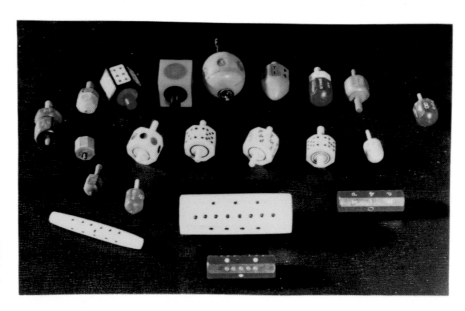

1920s: Cheating Devices A grouping of cheating tops, known as puts and takes, and "educated rolling logs" which were all "controlled" by any operator who knew how to use them. These were sometimes referred to as "gambling pocket pieces."

1932: K.C. and Mason Blue Book Art Deco style cover of "Blue Book" from the merged companies of K.C. Card Co. and Mason & Co. It contains 108 pages of cheating equipment and supplies.

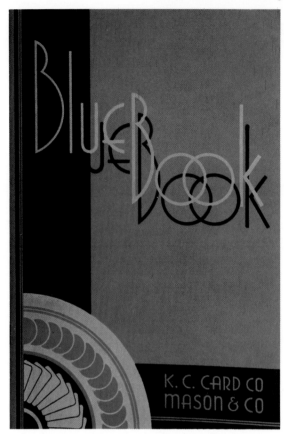

1932: K.C. and Mason Blue Book pages 46 and 47. These two pages show the various deceptive methods used for marking cards. Decks from well known manufacturers were "altered" and then repacked and sealed to resemble an untouched deck from the original factory.

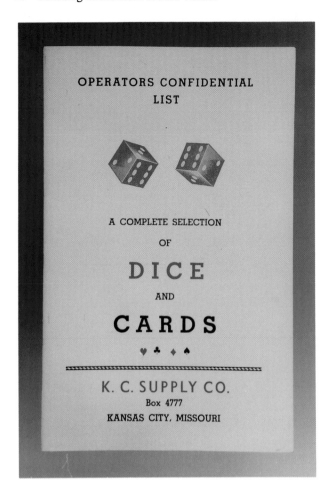

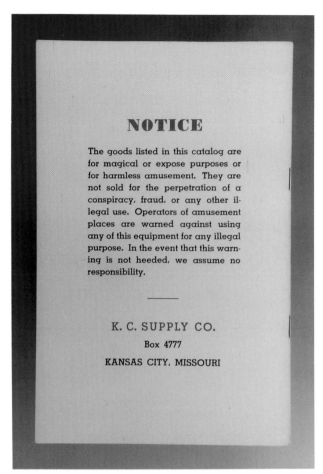

1930s: K.C. Supply Co. Catalog Cover of the 31 page catalog which offered for sale a large variety of cards and dice that could be used for cheating.

1930s: K.C. Supply Co. Catalog, the back cover. Statements such as these were utilized by almost all of the companies that manufactured or sold cheating equipment. This statement was an attempt to legitimize their products, claiming they were manufactured for other purposes.

1930s: Marked Cards Pages 22 and 23 of a catalog from K. C. Supply Co. of Kansas City, Missouri, shows how K.C. would use playing card decks from major manufacturers and mark them so that a criminal player would know each card from its back. The cards were then repackaged as if the box had never been opened.

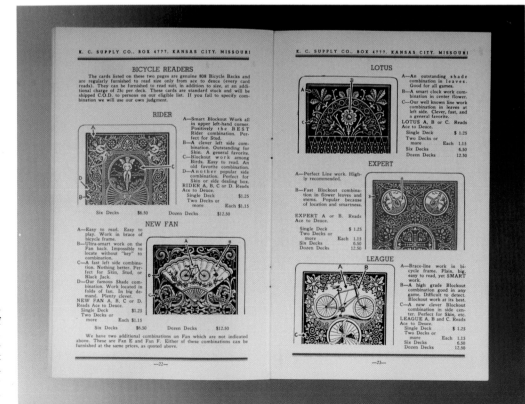

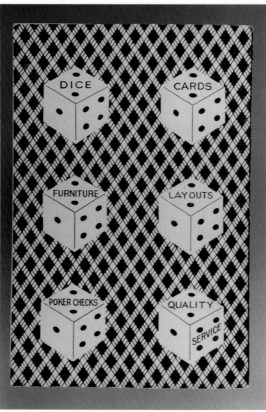

1930: K.C. and Mason Blue Book The covers of the 68 page catalog containing equipment that was nearly all intended for cheating, including carnival supplies, keyed punch boards, gaffed pharo dealing boxes and too much more. The ad on page 49 for the pharo dealing box boldly states, "Here again we show our ability to create a *money maker*. (my italics) Dealers can tell the third card coming. The gaff is perfect with no mistakes. Made and tested by men who know what is desired." While honest boxes sold for $25, this box that would deceive many an innocent player cost $200.

1930: K.C. and Mason Blue Book Inside front cover. Note the line near the bottom, "Our Blue Book is devoted almost exclusively to 'Special Work'."

Order Blank and Envelope Enclosed With 1930 Blue Book Although both names of Mason and K.C. were printed on this catalog of cheating equipment, the orders were directed to K.C. Card Co. in Kansas City, Missouri.

1935: Evans Catalog Cover of H.C. Evans & Company's 64 page catalog for "Club and Casino Equipment." Printed with black and silver ink on heavy weight grey paper.

1935: Evans Catalog, page 1. This front page of the catalog announces that, "Our machinery is the most modern, precision type and every workman employed by us is a craftsman in his particular line." This helps to explain why these objects are so beautiful and collectible today.

1935: H.C. Evans & Co. Envelope and Order Blank Don't try ordering a rosewood casekeeper with ivory markers for $25!

1935: Evans Catalog, page 64. This last page of the catalog shows an index of the various items produced and sold by H.C. Evans & Co., with a money back guarantee of satisfaction.

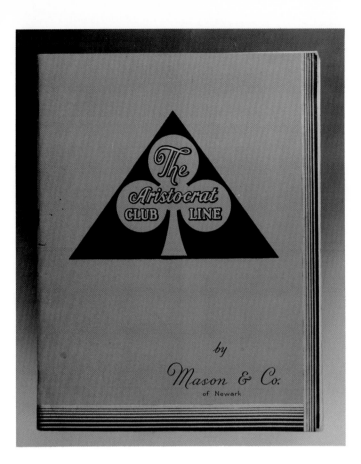

1930: Mason & Co. Catalog Cover of the 60 page Mason catalog from Newark. This particular group of Mason gambling supplies was referred to as "The Aristocrat Club Line" and cleverly used the playing card suit sign of a Club as part of the logo design.

1930: Mason & Co. Catalog, page 1. This page shows a photo of the factory building of K.C. Card Co. of Kansas City with its name still evident, alongside the Mason & Co. factory in Newark, New Jersey, suggesting a merger of the two gambling supply companies. Starting in 1930, they began to list the names of both companies on their catalog covers.

1936: Letter from Mason & Co. This letter was found in the 1930 Mason catalog and was probably the cover letter when the catalog was initially mailed. To quote Tom Kelly of Mason & Co., "Mason & Co. - manufactures everything used in connection with gaming - *either regular or special* - and a trial will convince you that we make it better." (my italics) Note the list, in the upper left hand corner, of seven major cities across the country where Mason & Co. factories were located at that time.

1932: Evan's Secret Blue Book Cover of an 80 page catalog. Nearly every page in this catalog was offering cheating devices for sale.

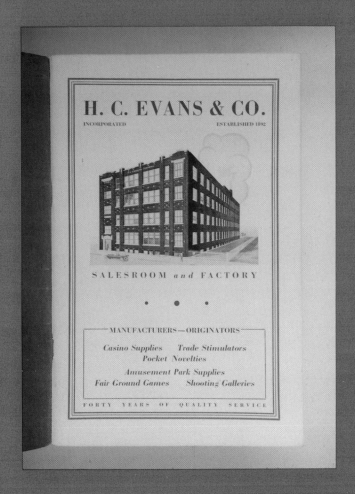

1932: Evan's Secret Blue Book, page 1. Shows Evan's factory and announces that the company began doing business in 1892.

1930s: Hand-Painted Controlled Roulette Wheel Made by H. C. Evans & Co. of Chicago. Along with other cheating mechanisms for roulette, such as wire and rubber bouncers or cork plugs, each to be placed in specific pockets of the wheel, Evans sold this roulette wheel made especially for dishonest play. It was "controlled" by the position of a single vertical screw in the aluminum funnel top. Where the ball landed was determined by the position of the top, as chosen by the croupier.

1923-1924: Evans Catalog Cover of a 64 page catalog that was distributed by H.C. Evans & Co. of Chicago. Although this company became one of the largest manufacturers of legal gambling supplies, they were also one of the largest manufacturers of cheating equipment.

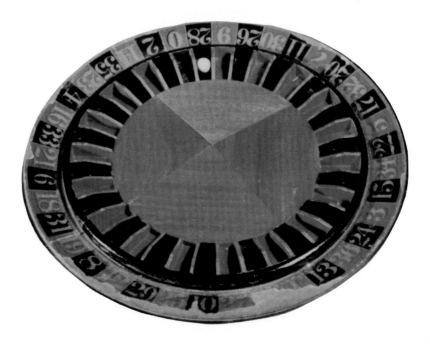

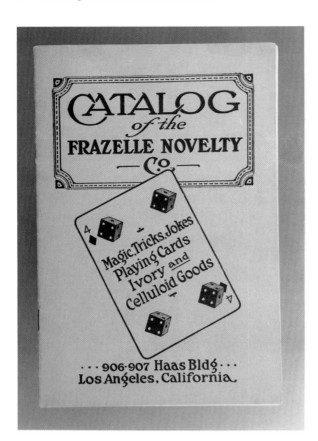

1923: Frazelle Catalog From the Frazelle Novelty Co. of Los Angeles. Despite the innocent sounding words on this cover, these 32 pages contain some of the most common cheating devices--loaded dice and marked cards.

c. 1935: Aladdin Catalog 48 page catalog from the Aladdin Specialty Co. of Chicago. Cover shows the Aladdin building framed by various types of gambling products. Along with the usual loaded dice and marked cards, they were also selling gaffed pharo dealing boxes, "daub," a colorless wax-like substance that was applied to the backs of cards during a game and was visible at certain angles, and "shiners," tiny secret mirrors that revealed the identity of each card as it was being dealt.

c. 1940: Code Novelty Catalog Cover of 28 page catalog from the Code Novelty Co. of Chicago which was offering loaded dice and marked cards for sale, alongside honest equipment.

1961: Catalog of K.C. Card Co. It appears that this "Blue Book" catalog was from what might have been the last year that companies like K.C. continued to do business on any major scale. In 1961, the Interstate Commerce Commission was given the power of new legislation, outlawing the transportation of these types of products across state lines. If any of these companies remain in business today, their former activities must be extremely small or non-existent.

1907: Shell Game Postcard Printed by D. Hillson. Cartoon pen and ink drawing of the notorious shell game. The man whose hands are quicker than the eye is shown with a nutshell head. The sheriff (note the star) is rapidly approaching.

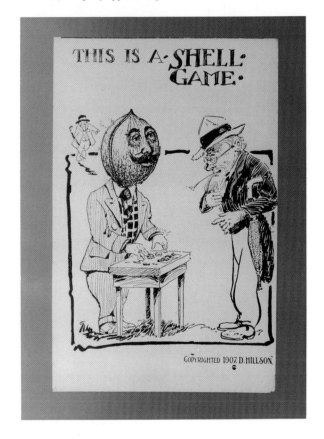

c. 1905: Three Card Monte Postcard The unwary customer has already pulled out his wallet, while the man on his right is reaching for his money. Note the man under the banner whose pockets have been emptied. The two men on either side of the dealer appear to be his cohorts who attract innocent players, a typical method used in this so often fraudulent game.

Gambling at the Gold Fields.

c. 1880: Gambling at the Gold Fields   Postcard published by the American News Company of New York. A pharo game with stacks of gold coins on the pharo board and in the pharo dealer's chip rack. The use of gold coins instead of chips was not unusual in mining areas of the early West.

GAMBLING IN GOLDFIELD, NEVADA.

1907: Gambling Room in Merchant's Hotel   Postcard using photo from Goldfield, Nevada. Printed by Gray News Co. of Salt Lake City. A game of pharo is being played at the lower left. An early version of craps can be seen in the booth at the right and a roulette table is on the left. A Mills Quartoscope and Regina Sublima, coin operated machines, are on the far right. Note name of Merchant's Hotel in reverse at rear window. The site of major gold mining activity, replete with dance halls and wild west saloons, Goldfield's population peaked to 30,000 in 1906, during its second boom (1902 -1912). Goldfield is almost a ghost town today, but not far from the new Tonopah casinos which capture the old gold rush spirit.

Chapter Six:
BUCKING THE TIGER

"Faro (pharo) has long been the favorite game of American gamblers.", says the 1864 *American Hoyle* (page 202).

Originating at about 1650 in France, the game of pharo became extremely popular almost immediately. It spread quickly to England and throughout Europe. By 1718, it had arrived in the colonies of North America, first appearing among the French settlers in New Orleans. One has to look no further than the crossed French and American flags on the ace of many pharo casekeepers and layouts to see that its French origin was well known.

Pharo playing had become extremely widespread in England, but was then banned by an Act of Parliament in 1738. However, it began to spread like wildfire in North America. From New Orleans, the French settlers made their way up the Mississippi, bringing the game with them to the present site of St. Louis in 1764. By the late 1760s, pharo had become a popular game there as well. Gradually, it began to be played up and down the Mississippi, as well as further to the east and west. Not long after the Louisiana Purchase of 1803, which included lands as far to the north as North Dakota, pharo became the most popular gambling game in the United States and the surrounding territories. Prior to 1864, it was common to play pharo with ivory chips, or even with gold coins when games were near gold mining towns.

The great popularity of the game of pharo continued until shortly before the beginning of the twentieth century. Western gambling halls put out signs with the picture of a tiger to let people know that pharo was played there. pharo soon became known as "The Tiger" and those who played the game were known to be "Bucking the Tiger". Records from the mining town of Leadville, Colorado from about 1878 tell us that there were 118 gambling halls at the time and that State Street, which was lined with gambling saloons, was known as "Tiger Alley". Doc Holliday was a pharo dealer at the Monarch Saloon in Leadville, while Frank and Jesse James spent time at Charlie Lowe's nearby. Doc Holliday also dealt pharo at the Oriental Saloon in Tombstone, Arizona, where Wyatt Earp was a part owner. Pharo remained popular because the action was fast and when the game was played honestly, the favorable percentage for the house was extremely small, estimated to be about two percent. "The Tiger" died a slow death and was still being played in Joe W. Brown's Horseshoe Casino in Las Vegas, Nevada in 1955.

My most difficult decision in writing about pharo was deciding how to spell it. Pharo, faro, pharoah, pharaon, pharoa had all been used in early writings. Although "faro" has been most commonly used since about 1850, a 1913 Webster's Dictionary explains that "faro" was "said to be so called because the Egyptian king Pharaoh was formerly represented upon one of the cards". But my own personal leanings toward using "pharo" were influenced by the playing card manufacturer Samuel Hart & Co. of Philadelphia and New York, which began to produce cards in 1848. Hart chose to print "Pharo" on the boxes of the pharo decks he started to manufacture in 1868. Hart's pharo decks were bestsellers for over 50 years, and were by far the most popular brand of pharo decks ever manufactured. However, either "faro" or "pharo" are acceptable spellings for this fascinating game.

Pharo required three people to manage a game: a dealer who also paid winning bets and gathered in the chips from losing bets; an operator of the casekeeper who kept track of the cards dealt; and a lookout or overseer who had probably been a dealer previously and now made sure the game was played according to the rules. Bets were placed by the players on any of the cards or combinations of cards on the pharo board. After shuffling the deck, the dealer placed it face up in the pharo dealing box. The top card was known as "The Soda" and had no part in the betting. The dealer then drew cards from the narrow slot in the box in a series of "turns". The first card of a "turn" was a loser, and any players who had bet on that card lost their money to the house.

c. 1890: Hart's Pharo Deck This square-cornered pharo deck was first manufactured by Samuel Hart & Co. of Philadelphia and New York in 1868. The absence of corner indices and the use of one way court cards were typical of Hart's deck, as well as all other pharo decks.

The second card of the "turn" won money for any player who had bet on that card. If two cards of equal rank appeared in one "turn" it was called a "split." When a split occurred, the house took half of the wager of anyone who had bet on that card. The game was made even more complex when players bet on combinations of cards, parlayed bets and "coppered" bets, which was betting that a card would be a loser. After 24 "turns," three cards remained in the dealing box, the loser, the winner and "the Hock". Bets were made on the order of these last three cards, which was known as "Calling the Turn".

Pharo equipment is extremely collectible but not very easy to find. There are casekeepers, also known as cuekeepers, made with card images and markers (sometimes of ivory) on rods, used to keep track of the cards dealt. The origin of the term "Case Card", which is still widely used in all card games, and refers to the last card of each rank, is derived from the way the casekeeper was used. There are also folding or straight boards, called layouts or spreads, that were made of green billiard cloth with cards painted on them, used for placing the bets. In addition, there are dealing boxes; chip racks; coppers; and decks of pharo cards. And of course, pharo collectibles also include scenes of pharo games.

Dealing pharo was done by hand until the mid-1820s. Because of cheating and card manipulation by the dealers, a method or device that would ensure an honest deal was desperately needed. Robert Bailey, a Virginia gambler and author, invented a pharo dealing box that was patented in about 1822. Bailey's box was entirely constructed of brass and the top was a solid sheet of brass except for a small hole in the center. This was to enable the dealer, using one finger, to slide the top card out through a narrow slit in the side of the box. However, the Bailey box was not well received because the top card could not be seen. In 1825, a Cincinnati watchmaker named Graves improved upon Bailey's design by creating a box with an open top in which the top card could be viewed.

Pharo dealing boxes that were based on Graves' design quickly began to be manufactured and soon became standard at games throughout the country. These are the dealing boxes most often found today.

But ironically, about one third of the few surviving boxes that we know of, were gaffed (altered) to enable the dealer to know the card beneath the top card, to slip out two cards at a time, or to employ other devious dealing methods. Eventually, gaffed boxes could be purchased directly from some of the pharo equipment suppliers. They were known as Sand-Tell, Side Squeeze, Lever, End Squeeze, Needle-Tell, Screw Box and other names. While the regular pharo dealing boxes sold for $25, the cheating boxes could cost as much as $200. These cheating boxes would, "Lock up to a square box", that is to say that they would bear the closest scrutiny by all players and could not be detected as cheating devices. Today, a gaffed dealing box is one of the most desirable and difficult to find of all pharo collectibles.

Casekeepers and pharo boards both have images of playing cards of an earlier era, and are thus more easily recognized by antique dealers as collector's items. Whether or not antique dealers know what they are, such items are usually assigned high prices. Casekeepers and boards are most often in the suit sign of Spades, with Clubs following a close second. Suit signs were of no consequence in pharo and a board and a casekeeper might be of any suit sign. However, it is a very rare pharo board or casekeeper that was manufactured with Diamonds or Hearts. If you find one of these red suit sign casekeepers or boards, you have just hit the jackpot. On the other hand, any piece of pharo equipment in good shape is a valuable find.

Chip racks and pharo decks are also a welcome addition to any gambling collection. A typical pharo chip rack would contain a minimum of 600 chips, and as many as 1500 or more. Pharo cards were one way court cards with square corners, and had no corner indices. Coppers were small octagonal discs, usually of red or black, placed on top of a stack of chips to bet that a card would be a loser. The name "coppers" was derived from the original use of a large one cent or smaller half cent coin for this same purpose.

Pharo artifacts are of intense interest to most collectors of gambling memorabilia since the game was so intricately entwined with the early exploration and frontier settlements of America.

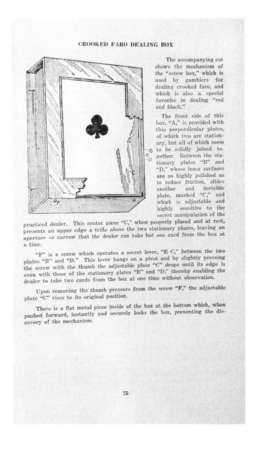

Don't be a Sucker - Cheating Exposed, page 75. This page has an explanation of one type of crooked pharo dealing box.

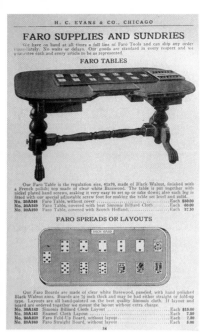

1918-1919: Evans Catalog page 54. From a 64 page H.C. Evans & Co. catalog featuring pharo tables and pharo "spreads" or layouts. Their best quality pharo board was $15.

1923-1924: Evans Catalog page 51. This page from a catalog of H. C. Evans & Co of Chicago, advertises the equipment they manufactured for pharo. It features a pharo table, along with boards, layouts and coppers.

1923-1924: Evans Catalog page 52. This page lists the German silver pharo dealing boxes and the casekeepers. Their rosewood and ivory marker casekeeper sold for $25. The decks of Pharo cards offered for sale at about $2 per deck were manufactured by Samuel Hart & Co., who began to manufacture this particular brand of pharo deck in 1868.

1930: Mason Catalog pages 20 and 21. This "Aristocrat Club Line" catalog was from the Mason & Co. factory in Newark, New Jersey. Note item G-1 which offered a deluxe model black walnut pharo table along with many other pieces of pharo equipment for $222.50. Listed on page 21 are G-9, Mason's German silver standard pharo dealing box for $25 and G-12, Mason's rosewood pharo casekeeper with ivory markers for $40.

c. 1860: Williams Pharo Casekeeper Manufactured by George Williams of 98 Elm Street in New York City, whose label reads "Williams Maker." This most unusual and attractive casekeeper is among the earliest known. It is fully enclosed in almost perfectly preserved rosewood and lined inside with a textured blue material. This is known as the closed type casekeeper because it is completely encased in wood, as contrasted with the later casekeepers that have open sections behind the markers, thus making them less expensive to manufacture. The card strips and maker's square appear to be hand-painted. It has red and white ivory markers and brass hinges. Measures 11" x 13.5" open.

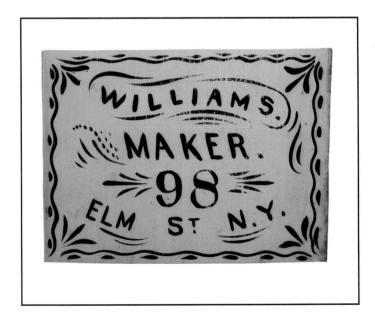

c. 1860: Close-up Detail of Williams Casekeeper Manufacturers label.

c. 1865: Pharo Casekeeper with Carved Cards Manufactured by Will & Finck of San Francisco. The most outstanding feature of this deluxe model casekeeper is the delicately carved suit signs on the wooden cards. Although the word "carved" is used to refer to this casekeeper, the "carving" appears to have been done primarily by the process of wood burning. The lines on the one-way court cards are also burned in, with the hand-colored sections more deeply incised. There are ebony strips between the cards and "fancy turned" ivory markers. The 12.25" x 13" frame is made of finely polished rosewood that is as smooth as satin.

Close-up Detail of Carved Cards Casekeeper A manufacturer's label from Will & Finck. This one is a single five pointed star with the name Will & Finck and the simple abbreviation "S.F. Cal" below it, all of this done by the same process of wood burning.

c. 1880: Will & Finck Pharo Casekeeper Manufactured by Will & Finck of San Francisco. The company of Will & Finck is one of the most sought after makers of gambling equipment, since they were in San Francisco and so closely associated with the days of the gold rush and frontier times of California. The beautifully designed, printed and varnished cards employed the suit sign of Clubs, the second most often used suit sign after Spades. Built of oak wood and with markers of composition, this one is 10.25" x 11.75" in the open position.

Close-up Detail of 1880 Will & Finck Casekeeper One of the numerous label designs used by Will & Finck, this one shows a rather long-necked eagle on a nest of young eaglets. The scale above them signified that their equipment was made for fair play.

Close-up Detail of the c. 1880 Will & Finck Casekeeper These delicately drawn and brightly colored court cards show full figures. These are known as "one-way" or "single ended" court cards, and preceded the "two-way" (mirror image) court cards which are familiar to people today.

1889: Samples of Pharo Cards Top: A page in a sample book from the Russell & Morgan Printing Co. of Cincinnati, Ohio which was used by their salespeople. Although many other types of decks were shown in this sample book, this page exhibited their "No. 366 Squared Faro" cards. Bottom: Another type of selling sample from Russell & Morgan for the same "No. 366 Squared Faro" cards.

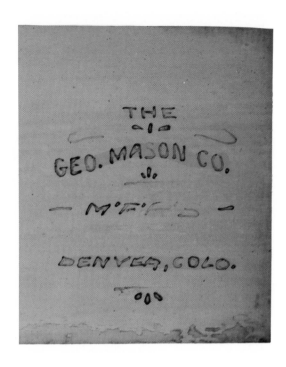

Close-up detail of the c. 1880 Geo. Mason Casekeeper Manufacturer's hand inked label.

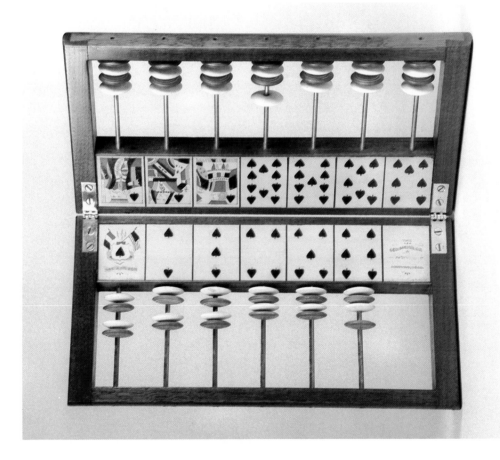

c. 1880: Geo. Mason Pharo Casekeeper Manufactured by the Geo. Mason Co. of Denver, Colorado. George Mason Co. is a close second to Will & Finck as a maker of some of the most sought after gambling collectibles. Deluxe model with hand-painted cards and ivory markers on a 13" x 13.5" frame of mahogany. French and American flags appear on the Ace of Spades.

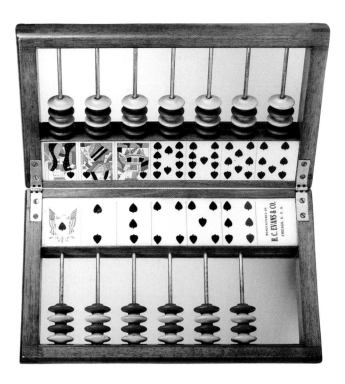

c. 1920: Evans Pharo Casekeeper Manufactured by H.C. Evans & Co. of Chicago. 11.5" x 13" oak frame with composition markers. The cards are on celluloid card strips. This company became one of the largest and most famous manufacturers of gambling equipment in the world.

Close-up detail of c. 1920 Evans Casekeeper Manufacturer's label.

c. 1890: Pharo Coppers Two full boxes of the tokens known as coppers, although these were made of a composition material and colored red and black. Coppers were used by players during Pharo games to reverse bets by placing one on top of the column of their chips on the board. A Pharo deck manufactured by Samuel Hart & Co. is lying on top.

c. 1895 No. 101 "Tigers" Card Box This deck was manufactured by the Russell & Morgan Factory of the United States Playing Card Co. of Cincinnati. This is one of the five brands of cards with which Russell & Morgan began their business in 1881. The other brands were "Army," "Navy," "Sportsman's" and "Congress." Choosing the name "Tigers" was due to the great popularity of Pharo which was known as "The Tiger."

Bailey Type Pharo Dealing Box Made by Mason & Co. of Chicago in the nineteenth century. The small opening at the top where the dealer was able to push each card out with one finger resembles the earliest style of Pharo dealing boxes, much like the type designed by Robert Bailey in 1822.

c. 1890: Ball & Bro. Pharo Dealing Box and Case Manufactured by A. Ball & Bro. of Chicago, this Pharo dealing box is silverplated, stamped with the name of the maker and the city, on the surface beneath the top on the open side. Shown alongside is an original hand-tooled leather carrying case for the box, with a hand stitched beige suede lining.

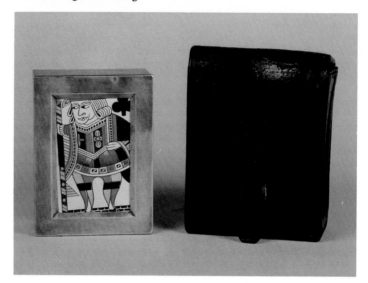

1920s: Pharo Dealing Box This box was manufactured in the waning days of the popularity of Pharo. It is made of steel and has no maker's mark. What makes it unusual is that the upper left hand corner is cut out to accommodate the corner indices. Shown with an Ace of Spades decorated with the Statue of Liberty and four Old Glories.

c. 1870: Will & Finck Brass Pharo Dealing Box Perhaps the only known Will & Finck Pharo dealing box constructed entirely of brass. Stamped "Will & Finck, Makers S.F., Cal'a" on the surface beneath the top on the open side. There is a Samuel Hart Pharo deck inserted in the box, held up by the metal band spring; the Ace of Spades is passing through the very narrow slot.

c. 1900: Mason & Co. Pharo Dealing Box Made of silver and stamped on the surface beneath the top "Mason & Co., Makers Chicago." Accompanying it is the original pigskin covered carrying case with a lining of red velveteen - slightly opened to show the gold stamp of "Mason & Co., Makers Chicago."

1890: Grote Pharo Board Layout for the game of Pharo which was so popular between 1720 and 1910. This board, 17" x 41", was manufactured by F. Grote & Co. of 80 Fourth Ave. New York City. The thirteen cards are hand painted on green billiard cloth which was stretched over oak, and framed with a one inch oak trim. The betting was done by placing the chips on or next to the cards.

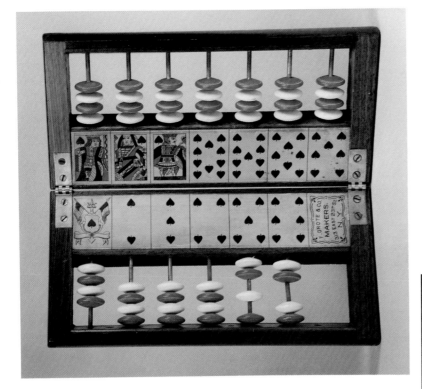

c. 1900: Grote Pharo Casekeeper Manufactured by F. Grote & Co. after they moved to 313 East 23rd Street in New York City. 11" x 12" deluxe model with ivory markers and rosewood frame. There are American and French flags on the Ace of Spades, commemorating the derivation of Pharo from its French ancestry.

Close-up Detail of c. 1900 Grote Casekeeper Manufacturer's label.

c. 1938: Land of Hunted Men Starring The Range Busters. Theatre Lobby Card from Monogram Pictures. A poorly researched scene that shows a game of Pharo without a casekeeper, an indispensable part of the game.

Above left:
c. 1950: Under Colorado Skies Starring Monte Hale and The Riders of the Purple Sage. Theatre Lobby Photo from Republic Pictures. There wasn't much that could stop a Pharo game in the early west, other than the sight of a lovely damsel in distress.

Above right:
c. 1940: Johnny Mack Brown Standing third from right in an 8" x 10" publicity photo, this well known cowboy actor is at a Pharo game in the Southwest. Noticeably absent from this Hollywood scene is the Pharo casekeeper which would normally be on the side of the table opposite the dealer. The famous roulette print "Double O" is hanging at the upper right. Before his days in Hollywood, where he began his movie career in the silent films of the late 1920s, Brown was an All American halfback at the University of Alabama.

left:
1943: The Woman of the Town Starring Claire Trevor. Theatre lobby photo from United Artists Corporation. Scene of an elegant casino and dance hall with ornate mirrors and crystal chandelier, but note the rough wooden plank floor and the sign on the upper right, "Check Your Guns Here." Pharo game at lower left.

1893: Oriental Saloon This turn of the century postcard was made from a photograph of the Oriental Saloon in Tombstone/Bisbee, Arizona, taken in 1893. The man in the left forefront is Tony Downs, part owner of the Oriental. The one seated comfortably on the tall chair next to the wall is the overseer, often called "The Lookout."

Postcard with Artist's Interpretation of Oriental Saloon Photograph This painting was probably done shortly after the original photograph. The unidentified artist has made creative use of his nostalgia for the Old West by painting much the same scene but dressing the players and spectators in more western looking clothing and adding a sign and some pictures on the wall. This painting was used in a Cyrus Noble Whiskey ad. (See advertising chapter)

c. 1900: Lovelock, Nevada Postcard Realphoto by Osborn of a Pharo game in a gambling hall in Lovelock, which is located between Reno and Winnemucca. It appears to be a very high stakes game, judging by the tall columns of chips on and between the cards, as well as in front of the players. The fellow seated in the corner was the lookout/overseer, working for the gambling hall to assure that the game was played correctly.

Early 1930s: Pharo in Reno Photo of a Pharo game in Reno, Nevada. The table is stacked high with chips, as the "lookout" sits on the tall chair overseeing the action. This is a rare scene, considering that after 1910 Pharo was seldom played, but these old timers are enjoying the game of their youth. After 1931, as the result of gambling being legalized in Nevada, Pharo had a brief resurgence there.

Early 1930s: The Grip of the Yukon Theatre Lobby Card from Universal Pictures. Scene from a crowded gambling and dance hall in the North Western Canadian territory. The deep concentration of the Pharo players in the lower right seems undisturbed by the music and dancing.

1930s: Pharo Bank at the Bank Club Photo postcard of Bank Club in Reno, Nevada. Photography by Frasher. C.T. Art-Colortone made only by Curt Teich & Co. Inc. of Chicago. It was difficult to find one Pharo game in the thirties but the Bank Club had two operating at the same time. This was undoubtedly an accommodation for their older customers.

1900: A PASTIME That Is Passing with the Frontier Photo postcard published by Newman Postcard Co. of Los Angeles. Although Pharo was fading in popularity by 1900, this game is going full blast with large stacks of chips bet on and between the cards. Barely visible are two "coppers" on top of two stacks of chips.

1910: The Last Deal Sepia-toned Realphoto postcard of a Pharo game in Reno, Nevada. Printed by L. Levitch. This was from the period that the popularity of the game of Pharo was waning, replaced by poker and other forms of gambling. The title, "The Last Deal" is thought to refer to the fact that the great old game of the early West was losing popularity, despite the intensity of the players and close ring of spectators in this photo.

Nineteenth century hand scrimshawed ivory chips.

Chapter Seven:
CHIPS PASSING IN THE NIGHT

Nearly all pharo and poker games prior to 1865 were played with ivory chips. On page 206 of the 1864 *American Hoyle*, we find this definition under the listing of technical terms used in pharo, "Checks [chips] - ivory tokens representing money, with which the game is played; they vary in color, size, and value."

Chips or tokens for use in gambling were designed to replace money throughout the playing of the game. Over the last few years they have become one of the fastest growing areas of gambling collectibles, especially casino chips and ivory chips. Yet I had never seen a catalog or any other publication before 1986, the time of the publication of *Antique Gambling Chips* by Dale Seymour, that even had an illustration of an ivory chip!

Very little is known about the manufacture of ivory chips and not one single factory has been identified. There are just a handful of c. 1880 catalogs from gambling supply houses that list ivory chips for sale. This is because: a) a successful substitute for ivory was invented in 1868; b) ivory items of all kinds, once extremely common between 1830 and 1860, had virtually disappeared by about 1875; c) it is likely that extremely few genuine ivory chips were manufactured after 1890; d) animal conservation efforts were becoming more widespread.

By 1880, ten years after the patenting by John and Isaac Hyatt of the first successful substitute for ivory, given the trade name Celluloid, items that had previously been made of ivory, such as piano keys, combs, kitchen utensils, knife handles, chess pieces, billiard balls, poker chips and hundreds of others were now manufactured from this new synthetic material. When other companies began to imitate this very first plastic, they used trade and commercial names for this ivory-like material such as French ivory, compressed ivory, ivoryoid, ivoryine and ivoride. Poker chip manufacturers were glad to take advantage of this new material.

Genuine ivory chips are individually hand scrimshawed works of art. There are easily discernable differences between chips of equal denominations in the same set, slightly different styles revealing the hand of more than one artist. The diameter of these chips generally measure one and one-half or one and five-eighths inches, with a few rare, larger denominations measuring up to two inches. Because ivory is initially porous and gelatinous, it continues to be sensitive to moisture, dryness, heat and cold.

Even a simply designed and common ivory chip will sell for $20. Almost any ivory chip scrimshawed with a numeral has a value of at least $50. Some unusual chips are worth up to about $250 and much more for a few exceptionally rare examples. Yet I have seen and heard of collectors being able to purchase large sets, sometimes over 500 ivory chips, for a very small amount. Treasures await lucky collectors who know what to look for - and know how to look.

Caution! There are reproductions and counterfeits in circulation. Most are old blank centered ivory chips that were scrimshawed sometime after their original manufacture. The inking in the center will be much more uniform on this type of counterfeit ivory chip. Despite the fact that such chips may be beautiful in their own right, these are not considered as authentic antique ivory chips. Once you are acquainted with this area of collecting, they are fairly easy to recognize.

Chips of other materials are also very collectible, such as mother-of-pearl, incised clay, bone, porcelain, metal, and even Bakelite. A most recent phenomenon is the collecting of chips from specific casinos. Some are chips from casinos which are now closed and some are older designs from casinos that are still in business. Contemporary casino owners would be very wise to attempt to make their present day chips as unique and beautiful as possible, and continue to create new designs, with the hope that they will become collectors' items and therefore never be cashed in at the casino.

Despite the fact that to many people, including some antique dealers, ivory chips look like plastic, to collectors and those who know, they look like gold!

In addition to the chips as collectibles, there are also fancy gaming boxes that were made to store chips. These were often beautifully and elaborately inlaid with exotic woods, metals or mother-of-pearl. They were usually neatly compartmentalized to include chips and decks of cards for poker. Boxes for pharo included extra compartments for a dealing box and coppers. Early professional gamblers carried this type of gaming box with them to ensure that they would not miss any opportunity to start a game of poker or pharo wherever they travelled. Such boxes were also used in homes and in small casinos.

c. 1860s: Largest Ivory Chip Known--Two Inch Diameter! This hand scrimshawed $100 ivory chip is among the most valuable of all ivory chips.

c. 1865: Pharo Gaming Box Made by Chubbs & Son, Makers to Her Majesty, London. Originally used by the Narragansett Casino of Rhode Island. Handsomely crafted box of mahogany with a frame of brass around the top, brass insets at corners, and brass hinges and locks. The hinged top is in two parts. The front part of the top folds open to show just the chip section, which contains 600 individually hand-scrimshawed ivory chips: 300 whites, 200 red 5's, and 100 blue bordered 25's. The front panel of the box also folds down for easy access to the chips. When the rear part of the top is opened, it then reveals the entire inside of the box. In addition to the chip section, it contains six compartments for decks of pharo playing cards and one compartment for the pharo dealing box, which also included ivory "coppers" (See Chapter Six -Bucking the Tiger).

c. 1875: European Gaming Box Exquisitely made box of ebony and scrimshawed ivory. Contains scrimshawed ivory chips and markers in compartmentalized sections.

c. 1890: Box of 300 "Horsehead" Ivory Chips Poker chip box made primarily of tiger oak. 13" wide x 9" deep x 5" high. Top of box has multi-leveled mosaic design expertly crafted with inlaid woods. It contains a set of 300 individually hand scrimshawed Horsehead design ivory chips: 125 white, 75 red borders, 75 gold borders, 25 blue borders. Also, narrow compartments for three decks of cards behind the chips.

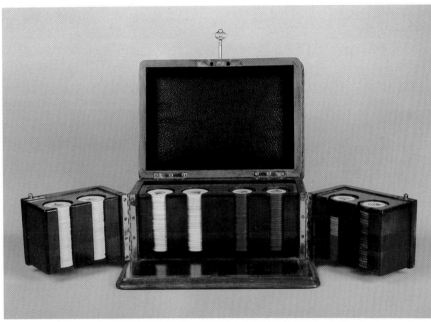

c. 1880: Hinged Box of 200 "Fan" Ivory Chips Poker chip box 10.5" wide x 7.5" deep x 6" high, expertly crafted of tiger oak. Each front section of this unusual box swings fully open, allowing easy access to the chips. These Fan Design ivory chips were each individually hand-scrimshawed. Includes compartments for two decks of cards.

Nineteenth century hand scrimshawed ivory chips.

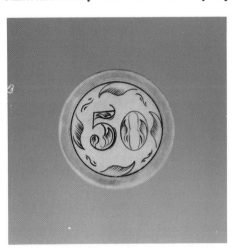

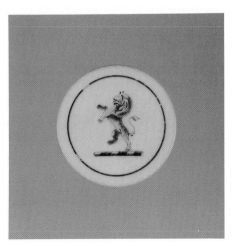

Nineteenth century hand scrimshawed ivory chips.

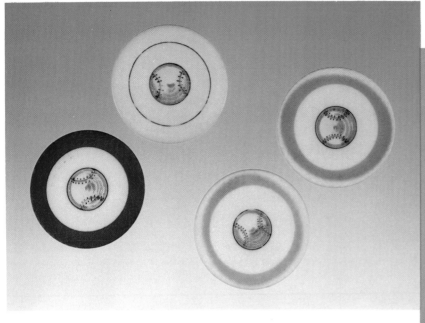

c. 1890: Poker Chip Box Perfectly crafted miniature of a roll top desk of tiger oak. Holds 250 chips in the wooden chip rack which can be lifted out by the brass handle. The two doors in the lower section of the desk each hold a deck of cards on the inside of the door. The roll top, as well as all the brass hinges and handles still work as easily as when this unusual chip box was first made.

c. 1880: Matching Ivories of Five Denominations From a set that is now represented by 187 chips, these chips, which range from values of one to fifty, sold for $13,200 at an auction held by Richard A. Bourne Co. of Hyannisport, Mass. in April 1990.

Nineteenth Century Hand-scrimshawed Ivory Chips.

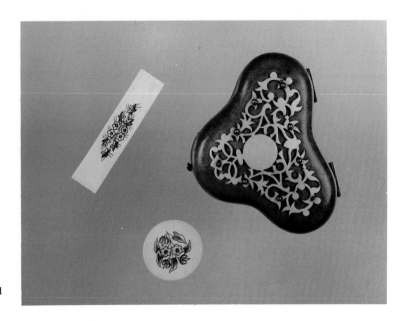

Nineteenth Century Gaming Box With hand scrimshawed ivory markers and chips.

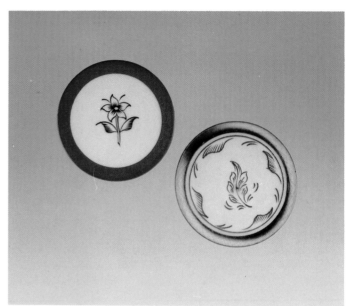

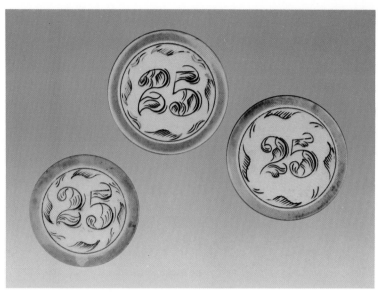

Nineteenth Century Hand-scrimshawed Ivory Chips.

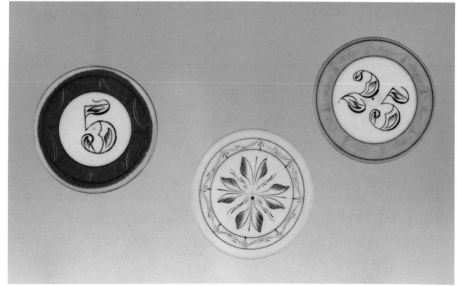

Nineteenth Century Hand-scrimshawed Ivory Chips.

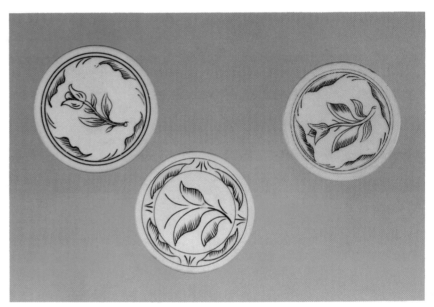

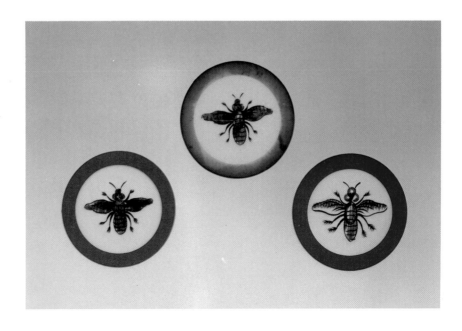

Chapter Eight:
HEY KIDS, WHAT TIME IS IT?

Whether based upon fact or fiction, the fancy pocket watch has become a symbol of the professional gambler. In stories and films these were often depicted as gold, encrusted with valuable jewels, and with gold chains long and thick enough to walk a dog! Such watches might also have had a practical purpose, since they could be used as ready assets.

"Gambling watches" is a loosely applied term to gambling games in a pocket watch casing, as well as to actual time pieces with playing card dials or gambling imagery. First manufactured in about 1880, the time pieces with playing card dials are the most highly valued of all of these watches. They actually kept time and were not used for gaming. Many of them were custom made and given as presents to devoted card players.

Almost all of the gaming watches actually used for gambling had themes of dice, horse racing, cards, or roulette. They began to be manufactured shortly after the playing card dial watches. Although the dice, cards and horse racing watches are fun and exciting to play, the roulette watches are the most popular among collectors of gaming watches.

Early examples of gambling watches, made from about 1880 to 1910, had clockwork mechanisms, porcelain or enamel dials, thick beveled glass crystals, and quality workmanship throughout. The watches of that period are the most beautiful and are quite difficult to find. By 1910, the gaming watches were being made with cardboard dials, cheap mechanisms, thin glass crystals, and were poor imitations of the earlier gaming watches. On the newer roulette watches, it was the dial that spun around and the pointer had been replaced by a ball.

A 1918/1919 gambling supply catalog from H.C. Evans described one roulette watch as, "An exact duplicate of the regulation Roulette Wheel. Comes in a handsome silver plated watch case; with this we also give you one fold-up layout, size 12" x 22". This game can be used for amusement or otherwise. Complete...$1.50". Many gaming watches, such as the one described in the catalog, were sold with paper or felt layouts so that actual bets could be made.

It is worth noting that the roulette wheels of Europe contain a slot for the single zero only, while the American wheels have one slot for the single zero and one slot for the double zero. This helps the collector of these watches to ascertain the probable location of the manufacturer of a roulette watch.

Because gambling watches are difficult to repair, the condition is a major factor in determining the value of any individual watch. Damaged ones are often worth much less than half of what the same type of watch would be if it were in good working order. All of the watches shown in this chapter are in excellent condition and working properly.

During the last decade, gambling watches have proven to be excellent investments, their value increasing many times over in just ten years. Values continue to increase as more collectors learn about their existence, and begin to appreciate the beauty of their designs and workmanship.

Hand-Painted Clock on Ivory Late nineteenth century image of the Queen of Hearts painted on a fine piece of ivory and set into a 2.5" x 3.5" bronze frame. Exceptionally well done detail and superb craftmanship. "La Dame de Coeur" (The Queen of Hearts) is inscribed on the back of this Swiss made clock.

c. 1890: Playing Card Watch with Hearts Manufactured by the New England Duplex Watch Co. The numbers from one to twelve are indicated by cards ranging from the Ace of Hearts to the Queen of Hearts, set on a pale blue background. This silverplate watch is slightly larger and heavier than other watches of this type.

c. 1885: Gambler's Pocket Watch The porcelain dial with cards depicting each hour of the day, includes all four suit signs. Since the hours of eleven and twelve were the jack and queen, the thirteenth card, the king, was placed just above the center of the dial. Tiny translucent red stones and dots of gold form a ring around the circumference.

Reverse of c. 1885 Gambler's Pocket Watch The back of this watch is inlaid with various metals depicting birds and flowers. This type of watch was often custom made and presented as a gift.

c. 1890: Custom Made Silver Pocket Watch Manufactured by the New England Duplex Watch Co. Each hour on the porcelain-glazed 1.5" diameter dial is depicted by a perfectly executed playing card, starting with the Ace of Clubs for one o'clock and going all the way around to the Queen of Clubs for twelve o'clock. Surrounding the cards is a circle of tiny raised dots of gold. The ornate initials of red, blue and yellow in the center read A. D. M.

Reverse of c. 1890 Silver Pocket Watch The raised initials N.C.G., and the engraved words, "Pro Patria Semper" (For Our Country Always), along with the "2" and "Co. A" suggests that this watch was given as a civil service or military remembrance to a devoted card player.

1904: St. Louis Roulette Watch This watch, made in the U.S.A., was sold at the St. Louis World's Fair which celebrated the centennial of the Louisiana Purchase. Gold plated with miniature roulette wheel marked with a zero and a double zero, a typical American type of wheel numbering. To activate the spinner on this watch, the knob was twisted rather than pressed down.

c. 1890: Card Roulette in Pocket Watch Case Silverplated with beveled edge glass. With a flick of the lever on the right side, the needle spins around and eventually points to a number, a card, a color and a suit sign. A bet could be made on any of these.

c. 1900: Cigar Trade Stimulator Watch This was an advertising piece for Barnes, Smith & Co., manufacturers of Fine Cigars from Binghamton, N.Y. You couldn't lose when you pressed the knob at the top and the clockwork mechanism spun the needle rapidly around the circle. It always landed on either one, two or five cigars. Probably given to tobacconists to be used by their favorite customers.

c. 1890: Roulette Watch Beautiful silverplate case with enamel roulette wheel that has a single zero. This 2.25" diameter watch with beveled glass is slightly larger and heavier than most others.

c. 1890: "Monte Carlo at Home" Roulette Watch The message on this watch suggests that the people can enjoy a game of roulette even when they are not at the Monte Carlo Casino. The enamel dial is a realistic depiction of a roulette wheel with a single zero. Gunmetal case with brass knob and loop for chain.

c. 1895: Little "Monte-Carlo" Roulette Watch An exact duplicate of a miniature roulette wheel with 36 numbers and a single zero. A beautifully enamelled dial with a gunmetal case and brass knob and loop for chain and a clockwork mechanism similar to other roulette watches.

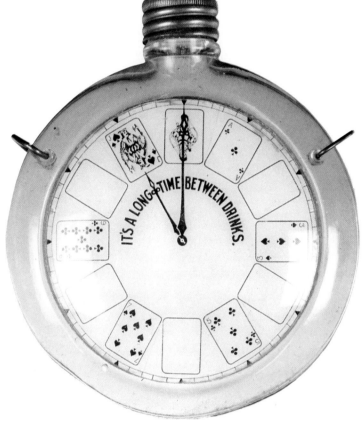

c. 1900: Paper Label Under Glass Flask The large round printed label embedded in the glass depicts a playing card dial of a clock, with the hands set at 11 o'clock. It perpetually announces "IT'S A LONG TIME BETWEEN DRINKS." The letters "U.S." are cast into the back of the thick clear glass flask.

c. 1895: Enamelled Roulette Wheel Beautifully crafted roulette wheel encircles an image of the Goddess of Abundance who holds a cornucopia in her lap. Each square and number are raised enamel on porcelain, as are the words Monaco-Salon Depose. A small knobbed stem on the top right side can be pressed down to make the pointer spin on the wheel, (using a clockwork mechanism) allowing a miniature, but actual game of roulette to be played. These watches were often sold with miniature roulette layouts on which bets could be placed.

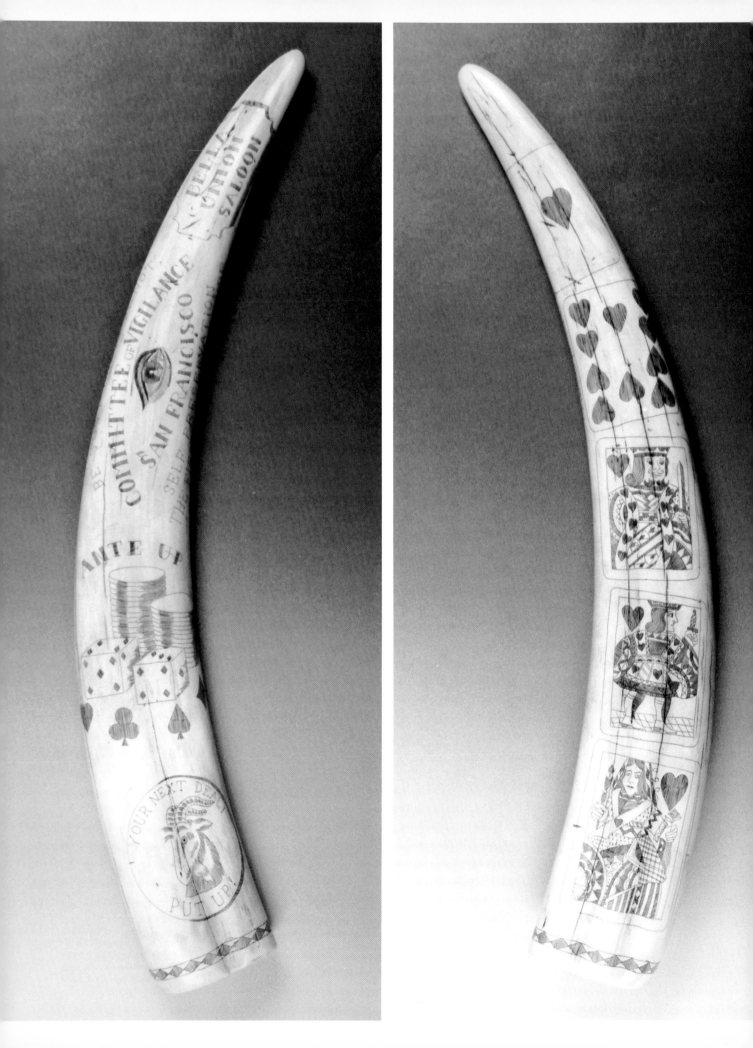

Chapter Nine:

WILD CARDS

Gambling collectibles that didn't require a chapter of their own, ended up here. Gambling collectibles have expanded into a vast variety of antique objects and more recent items of nostalgia. They often overlap with many other areas of collecting, such as magic, games, advertising, sports, brewery, tobacco, early western, politics, Civil War and other specific areas of American history. The truly devoted collector of gambling antiques will only be interested in an item if it is linked to gambling or playing cards in some way, and even within this parameter, many collectors will focus in on specific areas of gambling.

Nearly all collectors of gambling antiques, no matter what their particular interests within this field might be, like to collect visual images of those chosen interests. From at least as far back as the fourteenth century, artists have been fascinated with images of gambling and have created gambling and playing card scenes in oil paint, watercolor, pastels, charcoal, pen and ink, etching, engraving, scrimshaw and other art mediums. Some of the better known works are from artists such as Van Eyck, Hans Holbein, Paul Cezanne, Edgar Degas, Frederic Remington, William Aiken Walker and George Caleb Bingham. Old paintings and prints of gambling scenes can range all the way from extremely expensive art work done by internationally known masters to some excellent art that you might discover at a flea market. One very fine contemporary artist who creates still life paintings with playing

card and gambling imagery is Audrey Flack. And of course some of the most treasured images are early photographs *(See Chapter Two)*.

Paper ephemera constitute an important area of gambling collectibles. These are items that were produced to be used briefly and never intended to be saved. Much of the gambling ephemera that is now collected overlaps with advertising. This includes trade cards, which were an early form of business cards, posters, signs and brochures from playing card companies advertising their products, and any paper promotional and publicity items which depicted various gaming and gambling scenes. These were often used to promote liquor, tobacco, shaving materials and many other products. There are also tobacco or whiskey insert cards, greeting cards, theater programs, labels, tickets, stationery and order forms from playing card or gambling supply companies, instruction sheets from games such as "Roulette Cards," or the extra cards that accompanied decks. I have included postcards in Chapter Two, but they also fall into this category. Although not meant to be casually discarded, paper ephemera also includes items such as songsheets whose covers were decorated with scenes or designs that related to gambling or playing cards.

Lotteries have an extremely long history but lottery mementos are very scarce. Offering a cash prize was first instituted by the government of Italy in 1530, under the name of "Lotto." Lotteries of the early 1600s were used by the Virginia Company of London to finance the settlement of Jamestown. Kings College in New York, which later became Columbia University, started with a lottery licensed by the Assembly of the Colony of New York in 1746. Harvard raised funds for additional buildings with lotteries in 1774, 1794, and 1805. Money raised by lotteries in the United States was used to build schools, bridges, roads and for many other public and community purposes. Legislation was passed in 1894 that brought all lotteries to an end. The famous Louisiana State Lottery became the last legal lottery in the U.S. until 1963, when New Hampshire became the first state to institute a new legal lottery. Lottery memorabilia includes tickets and promotional materials. Collectors of contemporary lottery tickets make arrangements to exchange tickets with other collectors in as many of the states which now have legal lotteries.

Dice have the distinction of being the oldest of all gambling artifacts. Dice from 4,500 years ago were found along with inlaid board games in excavations of the civilization of Sumer (Southern Iraq). Dice are mentioned repeatedly in the ancient sacred Vedic books of India, where they were used in officially sanctioned gambling halls some 3,500 years ago. Small animal bones were used as dice in many cultures of the world; this origin is still present in the slang word for dice, "bones." The variety available in size, materials, colors of dice and dots, designs of the dots, inscribed logos and images, poker dice with images of playing cards, as well as the immense number of various types of cheating dice such as magnetic, weighted or altered edges, make this a specialized field in itself. Related items include layouts for the game of Hazard and Craps, Chuck-a-Luck cages, wooden dice drop

---

Opposite page:
c. 1851-1856: Bella Union Walrus Tusk An historically significant 17" walrus tusk whose carefully inscribed images and words hint at a period of San Francisco's most fascinating early history. Reports from San Francisco shortly after the beginning of the gold rush, tell of nearly 1000 gambling saloons in the area, giving rise to its nickname "The Barbary Coast." Many of the gambling saloons were on and around Portsmouth Square, the central plaza of this originally Mexican town.

This tusk was scrimshawed at the famous Bella Union Saloon and Gambling Hall located at Washington and Kearny Streets, directly on Portsmouth Square. It was probably executed by a member of the group known as "The Committee of Vigilance." This name is inscribed in the upper center of the tusk, over a watchful eye, and the words, "Self Preservation, The First Law of Nature" and "San Francisco." Above are the words "Be Just and Fear Not." At the tip of the tusk is a Bella Union Sign; at the base is a Poker Buck showing a horned ram and "Your Next Deal! Put Up!"; and in the lower center are dice, chips and suit signs with the words "Ante Up!." The other side of the tusk shows the expertly scrimshawed cards of a Royal Flush.

The Committee of Vigilance was initially formed in 1851 by nearly 200 prominent citizens who were concerned about lawlessness and the ineffectiveness of the local authorities and justice system in San Francisco at that time. Much of the chaos was caused by a very large influx of men who had escaped or been paroled from the penal colonies of Australia and were responsible for the major portion of the murder, robbery and arson during those years. The Committee of Vigilance continued to grow in numbers until it reached nearly eight thousand. In the Spring and Summer of 1856, the Vigilantes took control of San Francisco by force. They executed several criminals and expelled hundreds of others. The Governor of California finally regained legal authority over the city in November but by then many of the gambling saloons had temporarily closed, including the Bella Union. The Bella Union later became a well-known theatre and music hall until it was destroyed in the earthquake and fire of 1906.

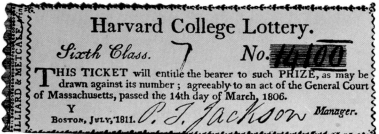

Eighteenth and Nineteenth Century Lotteries Left: This "Mountain Road" lottery ticket from 1768 is signed by the Father of Our Country, George Washington. Below: Harvard College lottery ticket from Boston, July 1811.

cups, and precision instruments to check the measurements and weight of dice.

Although wagering on horse races is as old as the pre-Christian Celtic myths of Ireland, collecting horse racing memorabilia is a fairly recent phenomenon. Some of the more easily found items are programs, photos, newspapers, magazines, posters, and of course parimutuel tickets. Items such as racing trophies and antique jockey uniforms are difficult to find, but parimutuel tickets from bets on the wrong horse are plentiful enough to wallpaper a house. Memorabilia from specific champions such as Dan Patch, Man O' War, Citation, Kelso, or Secretariat, or from races such as the Preakness or the Kentucky Derby, are some of the favorites of collectors. Horse racing carnival wheels, betting watches, games, and even clothing with horse racing motifs are also included in horse racing memorabilia. Items from harness racing and dog racing are also of interest to some collectors.

Many antique coin operated slot machines and trade stimulators are extremely beautiful and have been popular collectibles for the last two decades. They have been shown and discussed in numerous books, magazines, and periodicals. Some of the finest antique auction houses have had auctions composed entirely of these machines and there are antique shops around the country that specialize in them. Since this is such a large and complex area of gambling collectibles, it would be more helpful to direct the interested reader to Richard Bueschel's four volume set of *An Illustrated Price Guide* which covers antique slot machines and trade stimulators, as well as to other publications on this subject. *(See Contacts)*

Books are the foundation of most gambling memorabilia collections. I had originally planned to do a separate chapter on antique gambling related books entitled "Read 'em and Weep" but then found that it added greater clarity to place most of the older books and catalogs in the chapters on poker, pharo and cheating. However, quite a few other books about gambling are of interest. These consist of early books on the history of gambling or instructions on how to play specific games, manuals on systems and strategies, as well as biographies of famous gambling personalities, novels about gambling and even those nostalgia provoking publications known as comic books which depict gambling and playing cards on their covers.

In addition to the hand painted pharo and roulette layouts, which are very popular with collectors, there are also hand painted layouts from many short-lived nineteenth century gambling games such as Diana, Red and Black, Klondike, Hazard, and Hi-Lo. Early examples of these layouts were meticulously hand-painted on green billiard cloth and hand crafted with frames of fine woods. They are wonderful works of art that can be hung on a wall, or as some collectors have done, be placed under glass for table or desk tops. More recent layouts, such as those for Craps and Black Jack, though interesting and collectible, were usually mass produced with machine printed images on cheaper cloth.

Card tables produced by the finest early American furniture makers, sometimes made with inlaid woods depicting playing cards or suit signs, or with card motifs of needlepoint set into the center of the table, are extremely valuable. Early poker tables, pharo tables, roulette tables, and other gaming tables, are also desirable additions to any collection. Another type of object that was kept in homes or casinos were card presses. These were used to keep decks of cards from curling, bending or swelling when not in use. Much like the gaming boxes, presses were often made of fine woods, decorated with metals, contrasting woods, mother-of-pearl, or insets of beadwork.

Matchsafes and cigarette cases with gambling motifs are beautiful additions to displays of gambling antiques. Many of these were made of silver and decorated with insets of exquisitely enameled images. Before the invention of the now common safety match, metal matchsafes were made to hold wooden matches to keep them from getting wet or even igniting by accident. The need for matchsafes was virtually eliminated after the invention of the matchbook in 1892 by Joshua Pusey, a Philadelphia lawyer who was also the inventor of the roller coaster.

Some of the earliest examples of carnival wheels, spindle wheels, and paddle wheels were homemade and somewhat primitive. These nineteenth century wheels are now sold at leading antique shows and by antique dealers as examples of American folk art. In the 1930s, many exceptionally beautiful horse racing, dice, and playing card symbol wheels were commercially manufactured. A spindle wheel is much like a carnival wheel but lays flat on a table, usually with an arrow mounted in the center of the circle which spins until it stops between two of the small posts set around the circumference. The spindle games that have been found by collectors were almost always gaffed.

Casino memorabilia includes any item that was used by the many casinos which ranged from the grand elegance of Monte Carlo to small illegal gambling dens. This encompasses the lesser known casinos that were legal in nearly every state at different periods of history, as well as the more elaborate ones in Reno, Las Vegas, Lake Tahoe, and Atlantic City. This area of collecting runs the gamut from the Bella Union Casino in San Francisco of the 1850s to the new Trump's Taj Mahal in Atlantic City. It includes equipment, chips, ash trays, photos, postcards, promotional materials, newspaper articles, even swizzle sticks and matchbooks or just about anything that bears the name of the casino. One of the most unique items in this group is a scrimshawed walrus tusk from the Bella Union of San Francisco's gold rush days.

Another gambling collectible area is punch boards, which were large squares or rectangles made of paper and cardboard, on which the paper over each small hole was to be punched out, generally by the customers at shops where the boards would be kept near the counter. Some boards had as many as 2,000 holes. If the customer hit a prize hole, they would find a small piece of paper announcing their winnings.

Major prizes, though seductively illustrated on the board, were almost impossible to win. This was because shopkeepers could also purchase a "key" to let them know which holes contained the large prizes and to punch out as many of the prize holes as they wished before anyone used the board. These boards were often very colorful and graphic, relying upon drawings of glamorous women, sports, horse racing, or gold and silver coins marked with large denominations, to tempt the players.

Keno artifacts are especially interesting because the game of Keno was the predecessor to Bingo. In the last half of the nineteenth century, crowded Keno parlors operated in every large city. The game was played with 90 or 99 marble size ivory balls, wooden numbered cards, and an often elaborately carved "Keno Goose". The "goose" was a large wooden globe-like unit, pivot mounted on two poles so that it could be rotated to mix the ivory balls inside. When a single ball fell out of the hole in the bottom of the goose, it was called out much like the numbers in a Bingo game. The term "goose" was a reference to a goose laying an egg, and the game itself was sometimes called "The Golden Goose." An electronic version of Keno is still popular in Nevada casinos today.

Gambling and playing card games have left us with a huge array of objects that are of interest to collectors. Although memorabilia from poker and pharo are the most popular areas of collecting, artifacts from other games such as bridge, whist, euchre and cribbage are also widely collected. Trump indicators, whist scorers, and cribbage boards make desirable additions to a collection.

Objects of glass, ceramics, china or porcelain such as beer steins, plates, cups, ash trays, tip trays, lamps, vases, or other items that have symbols of gambling, playing cards, or gambling scenes, also enhance collections of gambling antiques.

Antique jewelry with images from gambling and playing cards were often custom made and given as presents to devoted card players or gamblers. These include cuff links, tie pins, money clips, belt buckles, rings, necklaces, earrings and bracelets, all of which can serve the dual purpose of being worn as jewelry as well as being additions to your collection.

Fabrics such as needlepoints, embroideries, linens, silks, and cottons with designs from gambling or playing cards are treasured by some collectors. Some of these fabrics were cut and sewn as pillows, card table covers, table napkins, or even used as wall hangings. Gambling and playing card designs appear on just about every type of clothing including underwear, jackets, shirts, pants, dresses, skirts, scarves, hats, neckties and suspenders, and some collectors enjoy wearing them as well as collecting them.

These are some of the wild cards in the deck of gambling collectibles. As you add these wild card items to your collection, you will become increasingly aware of how widespread the images of gambling and playing cards have become in our culture.

c. 1905: Mills Trade Stimulator This style of card machine, used as a trade stimulator in saloons, hotel lobbies and tobacco shops, was manufactured by the Mills Novelty Co. of Chicago and known as the "Jockey." The cabinet is solid oak. The name "Jockey" is symbolized in the elaborate bronze casting on the right side which shows two racing horses, the head of a jockey, and the lucky symbol of horseshoes. The cards on the reels form poker hands and the game could be played by up to three players, each using one of the three coin chutes. The payout for the winning hand was supposed to be in cigars, but was frequently paid out in money.

1958: Grand National Horse Race 10" diameter biscuit tin from Liverpool, England. Made by W. & R. Jacob & Co. Ltd., Biscuit Manufacturers, to commemorate the Grand National victory of D.J. Coughlin's race horse Mr. What, with jockey A. Freeman at the reins.

May, 1927: Lindbergh Postcard Published by George D. Duntze. Issued to commemorate Lindbergh's flight across the Atlantic, the back of this postcard says, "Captain Charles A. Lindbergh, the first aviator to accomplish a non-stop flight from New York to Paris." To honor the brave aviator, he was called the "Ace of Aces."

c. 1880: German Picture Frame Exquisite and unique frame made of inlaid glass and enamel. Images of the King of Hearts and the Queen of Diamonds set in a design of flowers and suit signs of Spades and Diamonds, with a Heart below and a Club reigning at the top. Heavy brass with brass stanchion on the back of the frame. The picture inside is an Ace of Spades from the 1824 Lafayette Deck manufactured by Jazaniah Ford of Milton, Mass. It features a portrait of the Marquis de Lafayette over a cannon and pyramid of cannon balls.

c. 1880: Matchsafe of Sterling Silver and Enamel The images of the cards inlaid in enamel into this 1.5" x 2" silver matchsafe show a Royal Flush in Spades; the meticulous details of the court cards and Ace are superbly executed. Note that there are no indices on the cards.

c. 1875: English Cigarette Case of Silver and Enamel An enameled Royal Flush in Hearts with no corner indices is inset into this 2.5" x 3.5" silver cigarette case.

c. 1880: French Cigarette Case of Silver and Enamel Initialed 3" x 3.25" silver case with slightly raised enameled roulette wheel on the top. Note that the ball has landed in No. 35. This cigarette case shows the single zero wheel of European casinos.

c. 1880: Silverplate Matchsafe Adorned with a bas relief of a multitude of chips surrounding a hand holding Four Aces and a King, an image reminiscent of the time when Four Aces was the highest hand in poker. The image on this 1.5" x 2.75" matchsafe is identical on both sides.

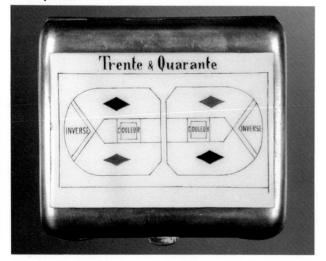

Reverse side of French Cigarette Case Shows the layout for the casino game Trente & Quarante (Thirty & Forty). The entire layout is enamel inset into the silver.

c. 1890: Sterling Silver Matchsafe Embossed relief design on 2" x 2.5" silver matchsafe depicts a wishbone, a four leaf clover, tumbling dice, gold certificates, stacks of chips and a Royal Flush in Diamonds. Wonderfully realistic sense of depth, especially on the corners of the dice.

c. 1880: "I'll Try Solo" Matchsafe Sterling silver and enamel, 1.5" x 2.25" matchsafe with a hand holding a spread of five cards. The image is enameled on the surface of the silver, with silver enamel bordering all of the suit signs. "I'll Try Solo" refers to the game of Euchre.

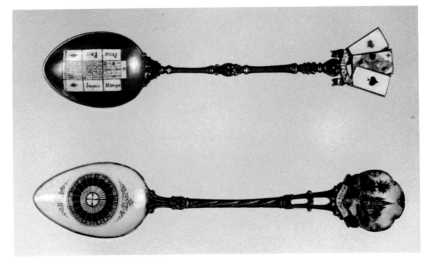

Above:
c. 1880: Monte Carlo Souvenir Spoons Exquisite workmanship of sterling silver with enamel. Top: An enameled Queen of Diamonds between two Aces over the words "Monte Carlo" on the top of the handle, and an enameled roulette layout in the bowl, perfect in every detail. Bottom: A painting of the casino at Monte Carlo over the words "Monte Carlo" on handle, with a single zero roulette wheel against a white background in the bowl- again, all in enamel.

Left:
c. 1880: Monte Carlo Souvenir Spoons Sterling silver with enamel. The spoon on the left has a perfectly detailed roulette wheel that can be spun on the twisted silver handle and a painting of the Monte Carlo Casino in the bowl, all in enamel. The spoon on the right also has a miniature enameled roulette wheel that can be spun, but this one has a pointer to determine the winning number. Blue and white enamel is set into the handle and there is an enameled scene of the casino and surrounding area of Monte Carlo in the bowl.

Right:
c. 1880: Monte Carlo Souvenir Spoons Sterling silver with enamel. Roulette wheels that actually spin on handles, enameled scenes of casino in bowls.

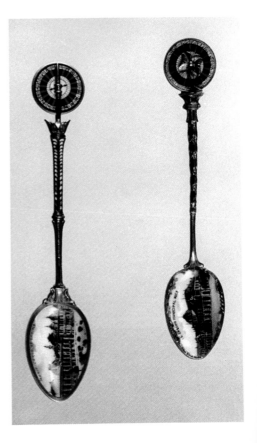

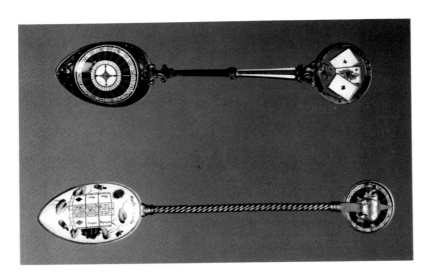

c. 1880: Monte Carlo Souvenir Spoons Silver with enameled playing cards; roulette wheel, roulette layout, and a tiny pig for good luck.

1885: The House of Cards A charming engraving from Florence Gravier, artist M. Klinkisht. Printed in a German magazine in 1885.

c. 1960: Laundry Line of Cards From Citta di Carte (City of Cards) set of 12 dishes made by Fornasetti of Milan, Italy. Each 10" diameter dish wittily employs playing card images in a different surrealistic design. Many of the card images are architectural, such as in the center left of this dish. Some of the dishes use cards to create skyscrapers; others show cards as part of more natural scenes such as rivers or mountain paths.

c. 1890: Wall of Fives Oil on canvas, 8" x 10" painting of a five dollar bill and five cards that make up a Royal Flush. The background wall is painted to look like a sheet of wooden planking with nails hammered in. The five dollar bill is marked "The series of 1880" and shows President Andrew Jackson, a well known gambler, who is now on 20 dollar bills.

Chuck-a-Lucks, Dice and Hazard Dice Drops This group includes two chuck-a-luck cages on the top left, several perfectly lathed dice drops for the game of Hazard on the top right, and three sets of poker dice, one of Pyralin which was one of the first trade names used for celluloid when it began to replace ivory in the 1870s.

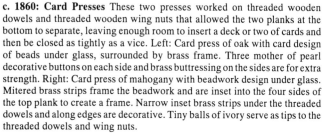

c. 1860: Card Presses These two presses worked on threaded wooden dowels and threaded wooden wing nuts that allowed the two planks at the bottom to separate, leaving enough room to insert a deck or two of cards and then be closed as tightly as a vice. Left: Card press of oak with card design of beads under glass, surrounded by brass frame. Three mother of pearl decorative buttons on each side and brass buttressing on the sides are for extra strength. Right: Card press of mahogany with beadwork design under glass. Mitered brass strips frame the beadwork and are inset into the four sides of the top plank to create a frame. Narrow inset brass strips under the threaded dowels and along edges are decorative. Tiny balls of ivory serve as tips to the threaded dowels and wing nuts.

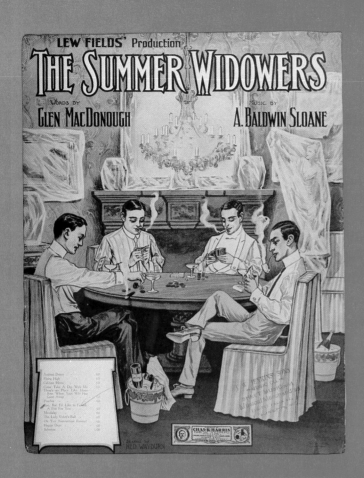

1910: Songsheet Printed by Charles K. Harris at Broadway and 47th Street in New York. Painting by Starmer on a cover of sheet music from a song in the Lew Fields Production of the "The Summer Widowers." All the wives have gone away for the summer and the husbands get together for the familiar combination of smoking, drinking and a friendly game of poker.

c. 1920: "The National Game" Punchboard An illustration of a poker game on top, again indicating that poker was thought of as the most popular American game. Customers could choose a specific peg hole and from it they would receive a tiny piece of paper which told them the hand they drew--and the number of prize points they won with it. This 4.25" x 5.75" punchboard has never been used.

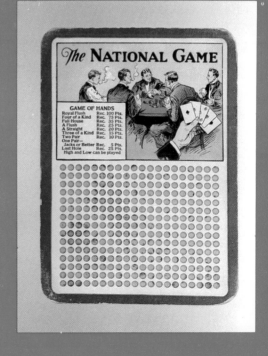

1888: Two Baseball Playing Cards From a set of 72 cards. Each of the eight National League teams of 1888 are represented by nine cards, a player at each position. Note the miniature playing cards in the right hand corners. These are for a game and cannot be used as a standard deck, since there are no 2's, 3's, 4's or 5's.

Nineteenth Century Lotteries Top: Ticket from the Honduras National Lottery Co. Drawing was held at Puerto Cortez on July 10th, 1894. First Prize $75,000!! Bottom: Ticket from Louisiana State Lottery Co. of New Orleans and Kansas City, Kansas. The drawing was held in Kansas City, Kansas on October 9th, 1894.

Nineteenth Century Lotteries Left: Lottery advertising card for the benefit of Henry College. Drawing in Covington, Kentucky on February 28th, 1884. First Prize $30,000. Right: An advertisement for the, "Fairest Lottery in the World." From Commonwealth Distribution Co. Monthly lottery drawings in Louisville, Kentucky. First Prize $30,000.

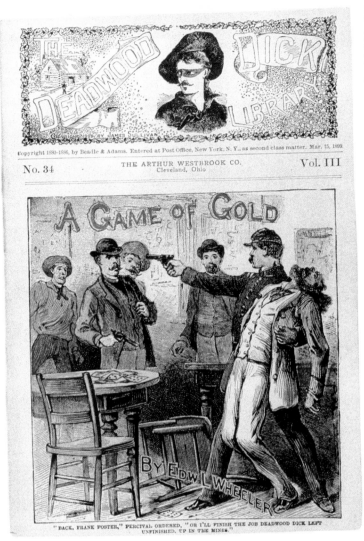

1899: A Game of Gold by Edward L. Wheeler. Published by the Arthur Westbrook Co. of Cleveland, Ohio. 5.25" x 7.5" soft cover pulp booklet of 31 pages. This is No. 34 of The Deadwood Dick Library which consisted of 64 similar publications, all featuring this heroic figure of the early West. Some people believe Deadwood Dick was a fictitious character, but most think he actually existed. In fact, various people have claimed to be the original Deadwood Dick.

1946: The Finger Man by mystery writer Raymond Chandler. Roulette imagery in a painting by Lionel Gelb is printed on this soft cover, 5.5" x 7.5" book. It was the 43rd issue of a series entitled "Murder Mystery Monthly," published by Avon Book Co. of New York in 1946. Chandler was the author of "The Big Sleep" and many other mystery stories.

1956: The Last Chance 190 page paperback by Frank O'Rourke. Published by Dell Publishing Co. of New York. Cover painting by John McDermott. The story of a professional gambler trying to settle down in a small western town, but finding that "He had to leave his mark. That was in the cards..."

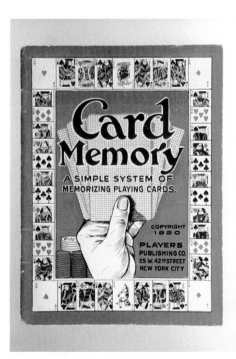

1937: Worth in Gold by Nathan Wolfson. Printed in U.S.A. An 87 page, paper cover book, 6" x 9.25", describing systems that the author suggests will help to win in various games. Listed among the numerous games of chance he covers, Wolfson includes the "Stock Exchange and Board of Trade."

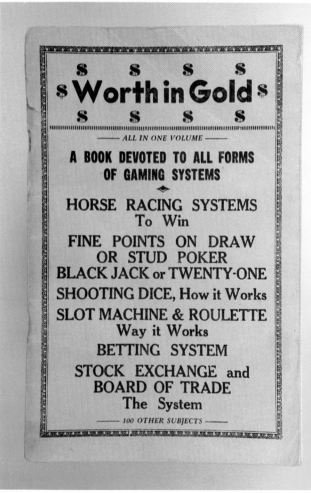

1920: Card Memory A 32 page, 4.5" x 6" paper cover booklet published by Players Publishing Co. of New York. I read this book from cover to cover but can't remember a thing about it.

1889: The New Book of Hoyle's Games Royal Publishing Co. of Philadelphia. 5" x 7" paper cover book of 159 pages. Of all the many games included in the book, the publisher chose the poker hand of a Royal Flush for the printed cover illustration, reinforcing the idea that poker was the most popular card game of the period.

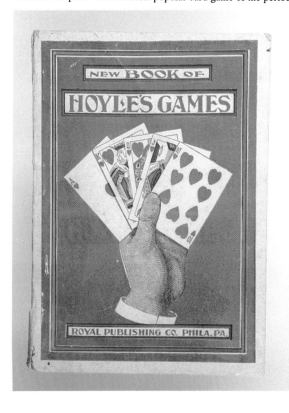

1905: Card Rules Published by Wehman Bros. of New York. Soft cover, 4.5" x 7" book of 179 pages. Title page calls this book "Hoyle's Card Games: Standard Rules for Playing All Card Games." Contains the rules for over 100 card games, including Draw Poker, Pharo, Brag, Whist and Sancho Pedro. Distributed free, compliments of B. Stern & Son, a New York City Department Store.

Opposite page:
December, 1946/January, 1947: Black Cat Comics, Vol. 1 No. 3 Published by Home Comics, Inc. of St Louis, Missouri. Harvey Publications. The Black Cat was one of the first comic book heroines, the tales of this "glamorous Hollywood detective" are said to have originated in 1941. This cover shows her raiding a roulette game at a casino.

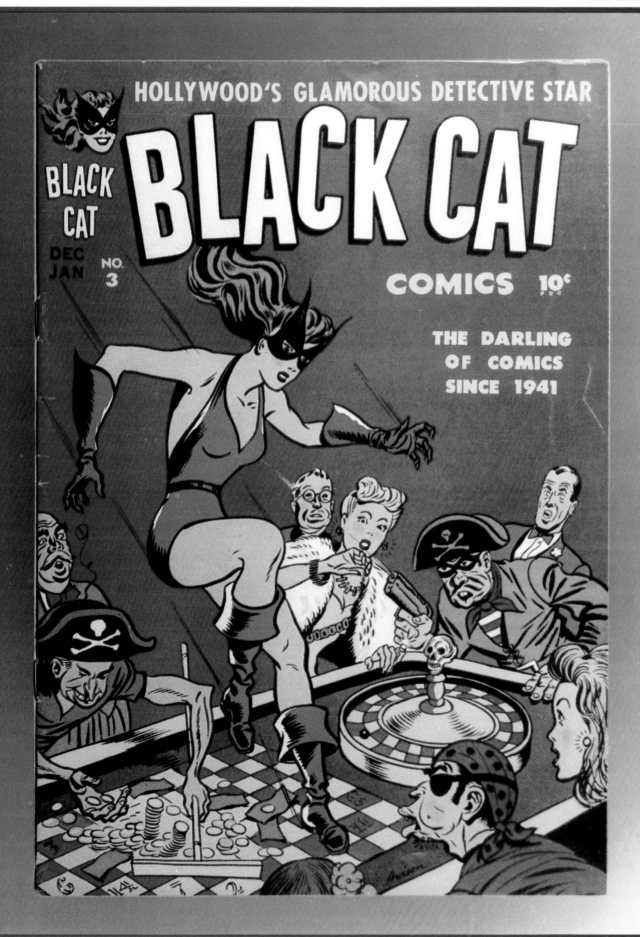

May/June, 1952: Racket Squad in Action, Vol.1 No.1 Charlton Comics Group of Derby, Connecticut. This is the first issue of what became a series of 29 bi-monthly issues. It was the only comic book series devoted exclusively to exposing cheating, confidence games, swindles, frauds, and other rackets. It featured the fictitious Inspector J.J. O'Malley, who exposed and arrested those who cheated others. On this cover illustration, painted by Tyler Forgione, a plain clothes O'Malley is bringing a halt to a crooked three shell game at a carnival. One of the two editors of this series was Walter Gibson, a prolific author of countless articles and books on magic, gambling and cheating. He was also a writer on "The Shadow" series, one of the most successful radio shows of all time.

July/August, 1952: Racket Squad in Action, Vol.1 No. 2. Charlton Comics Group of Derby, Connecticut. Cover art by Albert Tyler. This second issue of Racket Squad contains "Dice Games Exposed" written by Sidney Radner, a good friend of mine who has spent a lifetime exposing crooked gambling and has authored many books on the subject.

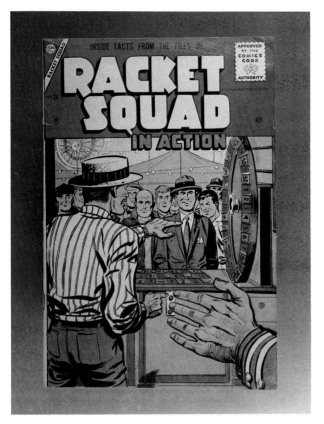

February, 1957: Racket Squad in Action, Vol.1 No. 24. Charlton Comics Group of Derby, Connecticut. This cover shows a carnival wheel controlled by the operator whose finger waits at the button. The "long arm" of Inspector J.J. O'Malley is about to put a stop to this deception.

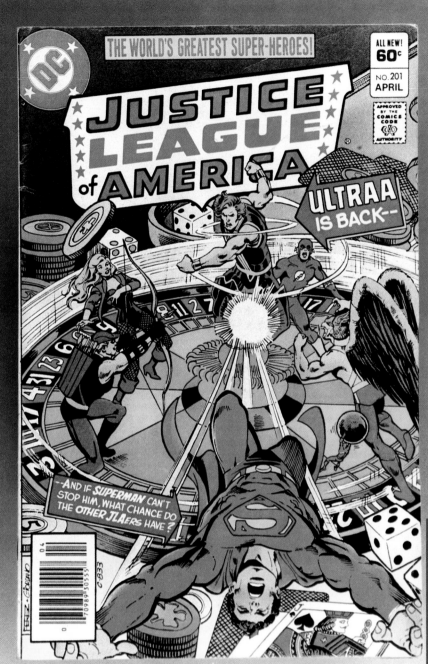

April, 1982: Justice League of America Comic book by D.C. Comics, Inc. of New York. Cover drawn by Perez and Giordano. Although Superman seems to be having a terrible time at the moment, it would be a safe bet that he'll win in the end. Note playing cards, poker chips and dice around the roulette wheel.

October/November, 1950: Gang Busters Comic Book, No. 18 Published by National Comics Publications of New York. A dramatic and creative illustration of two policeman capturing two members of The Black Ace Gang. Beneath the photo is the familiar refrain, "You can't beat the law!"

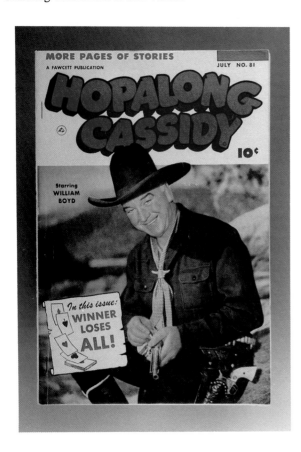

July, 1953: Hopalong Cassidy Comic Book, No. 81 Published by Fawcett Publications of Greenwich, Connecticut. The feature story entitled "Winner Loses All," is announced on the cover with a scroll showing four aces.

November, 1958: Sheriff of Tombstone, Vol.1 No.1 Comic book published by Charlton Comics Group of Derby, Connecticut. Young Luke Spade becomes the sheriff and breaks up the unlawful activities going on at the Royal Flush Saloon.

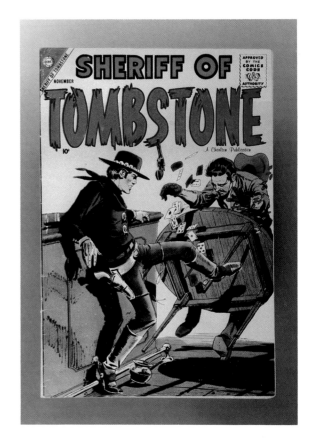

February, 1970: Kid Colt Outlaw Comic book published by Magazine Management Co. of New York. Cover illustration by J. Severin. Cards and poker chips went flying as the poker table was overturned by the arrival of Kid Colt with his gun blazing.

September, 1965: Boris Karloff Tales of Mystery Comic book published by K. K. Publications of Poughkeepsie, New York. The King, Queen and Jack from a Royal Flush lying on the table have come alive and are about to revenge themselves on Mr. Karloff for marking the cards.

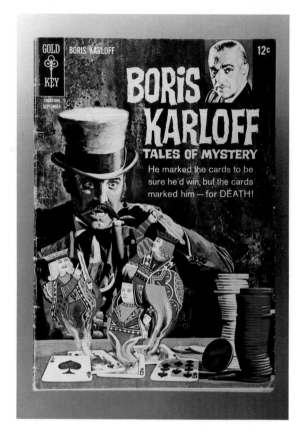

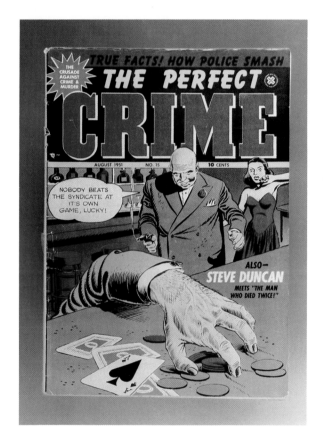

August, 1951: The Perfect Crime Comic book by Cross Publications, Inc. of New York. Cover illustration portrays the hand of a man who is nearly dead, yet still trying to take the chips in the pot with him.

October, 1962: House of Mystery Comic Book published by National Periodical Publications of Sparta, Illinois. The cover depicts a cosmic game of cards in which humans are being used for betting purposes by extra terrestrials.

May, 1975: Dennis the Menace Comic book published by Fawcett Publications of Greenwich, Connecticut, drawn by Hank Ketcham. Under the subtitle of "Big Deal," we see Dennis as the Ace of Spades, flanked by his mother, the Queen of Hearts and his father, the King of Clubs.

March, 1962: Mad Magazine Published by E.C. Publications of New York. Cover illustration by Kelly Freas. This photograph is humbly dedicated to William M. Gaines, creator, founder and publisher of Mad Magazine. Mr. Gaines passed away in 1992. Also to Harvey Kurtzman, artist and co-creator of Mad Magazine, who passed away in 1993. They are both fondly remembered as men who stood tall while others bowed.

Chapter Ten:
SHUFFLE, CUT AND DEAL ME IN

The Chinese encyclopedia *Ching Tze Tung* published in 1678 dates the invention of playing cards to 1120 A.D. in China, although an early collector of books about poker and gambling, Judge Oliver P. Carriere of New Orleans, asserted that the game of As Nas was played in 2000 B.C. in the area of present day Iran.

Since their initial development, playing cards have been associated with chance, fate, fortune-telling, magic, games and gambling. They appear to have evolved from the use of natural objects such as bones, nuts, rocks, leaves, sticks or shells. In early times, the chance arrangements of these objects when tossed or thrown, were used to indicate possible events in the future, and these objects also became the origins of various games.

The earliest cards were printed with wood blocks on rag or rice paper, or were hand painted on lacquered wood disks. Some cards were actually pieces of paper money printed in the Tang Dynasty of China which reigned between the seventh and the tenth centuries. The first European playing cards appeared in Italy at about 1300, believed to have been brought there by nomadic Gypsies from India or by Arabs from Northern Africa. For a few centuries, playing cards in Europe were the exclusive domain of the aristocracy, and were always individually hand painted. Originally, only the royalty and nobility passed their time in this newly discovered pleasurable amusement. The court cards, Kings, Queens and Jacks (Knaves), still reflect the early vanity of the ruling class.

Playing cards appeared in France at about 1360. The standard suit sign symbols used in the United States today, spades, hearts, diamonds, and clubs, were first designed by the French. These four suit signs originally represented the four divisions of society, spades as royalty and the military, hearts as clergy or priesthood, diamonds as merchants, and clubs as the peasantry. This representation of a class or caste system, as symbolized by the four suits, which was common in all European cards no matter which specific symbols were used, may hint at the origins of suit signs on cards being from the ancient Indo-European four caste systems of India and Iran, which were almost identical in structure. The oldest known playing card ever found, believed to be from the tenth century, was discovered in the far western Turfan district of China. However, it is interesting that this exact area of China was inhabited by a group of Indo-European people in the tenth century and that the first playing cards may have been developed two centuries earlier than the date given in the Ching Tze Tung encyclopedia.

Since playing cards had arrived in Europe almost 200 years before the voyage of Columbus in 1492, and the use of wood block printing had eventually brought them into more common usage all throughout Europe, it is likely that the sailors on the ships commanded by Columbus brought playing cards with them to the Americas. Garcilaso de la Vega wrote in his *Historia de la Florida* that soldiers from a Spanish expedition to the Americas in 1534 played with cards of leather. Old cards of the Spanish style, made of deerskin and sheepskin, have been found among American Indian tribes of the Southwest.

December, 1885: Calendar Sheet 5" x 9.5" Printed by The Russell & Morgan Printing Co. of Cincinnati, Ohio, the manufacturers of United States Playing Cards. Note the playing cards on the Christmas tree. This was only four years after this now well known company had formed as a business. These calendars were issued from about 1882 to 1894, but less than a handful of complete calendars are known to exist today.

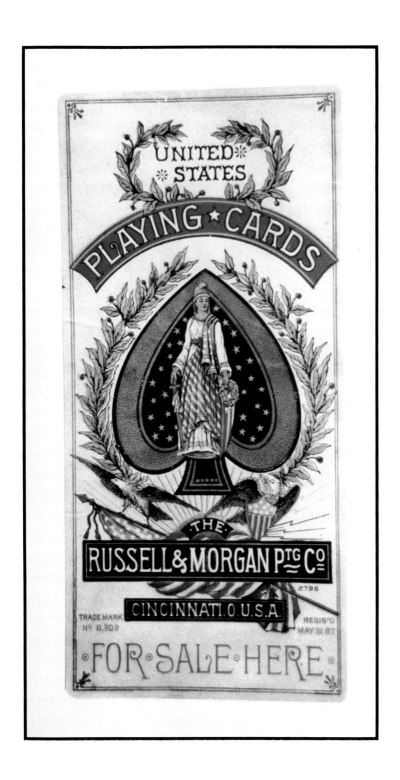

1890: Russell & Morgan/USPC Trade Card
Colorful, 3.5" x 7" trade card from the Russell & Morgan Printing Co. as it began to use the new name of United States Playing Cards. These were distributed free to the retail stores which carried their products, to promote sales. The patriotic theme is expressed in the clothing of the "Lady Liberty" figure, as well as in the flag, shield and eagles.

In addition to the Spanish cards, in 1606 English cards were brought to Jamestown by the English settlers, and shortly thereafter cards were brought to New Amsterdam (New York) by Dutch settlers. Playing cards also found their way into Puritan New England, revealed by a Plymouth Colony record of 1633, stating that several people were fined two pounds each for playing cards. By 1656 there was a Plymouth Colony penalty of forty shillings for anyone caught playing cards, and "for the second offence to bee publickly whipt." Until 1700, there were strict laws and severe penalties for participating in horse racing, billiards, cock-fighting, ten-pins, and for playing with dice or cards.

By 1720, playing cards were listed for sale by stationers, bookbinders and other dealers of paper goods in the colonies. By 1750, card playing had become somewhat more acceptable and decks of cards were advertised in the newspapers. However, it was illegal to manufacture cards in the colonies, and these cards were almost always imported from England. The stream of new immigrants brought many types of decks with them. These decks contained either 32, 36, 40 or 48 cards and had been manufactured in England, France, Germany, Spain, Italy or Austria.

Not only was it illegal to manufacture cards in the colonies but the British government levied a tax on decks of playing cards with the Stamp Act of 1765. It decreed: "And for and upon every pack of playing cards which shall be sold or used within said colonies or plantations, the several stamp duties following: for every pack of such cards, the sum of one shilling." Also, "Be it further enacted that from and after the first day of November 1765, no playing cards shall be sold or used in play within said colonies and plantations unless the paper and thread enclosing them shall have been sealed and stamped as provided in pursuance of this act." (As a school boy I was taught that it was the tax on tea that caused the Boston Tea Party and the American Revolution, but perhaps it was the tax on cards that aroused the spirit of independence among the colonial card players.)

The first manufacturer to produce playing cards in the U.S. is believed to have been Jazaniah Ford of Milton, Mass. The Ford decks that have so far been discovered date back to c. 1790. But it was quite likely that Mr. Ford had competition even at that time, notably from Amos Whitney of Boston, Massachusetts, and Thomas Crehore of Dorchester, Massachusetts.

As more and more companies in the United States began to make and sell cards, a number of innovations were made in the designs. The two-way reversible court cards were first developed in the 1830s but did not really begin to replace the one-way full figured court cards until the 1870s. Jokers first appeared in the 1860s. Corner indices were added by Samuel Hart & Co. (Saladee's Patent) in 1864. Other innovations, such as using patriotic symbols for the suit signs, a variety of designs for the court cards, introducing new colors for the four suit signs, and creating more than four suits, were often tried but never gained any general acceptance.

Decks of playing cards are often miniature works of art, and the immense diversity of deck designs created over the centuries, offer a collector a never ending source of information, pleasure and challenge.

c. 1905: New York Consolidated Trade Card The New York Consolidated Card Co. started their business in 1871. In this witty illustration on a promotional trade card, the cards are playing cards. It seems to be a game of poker with columns of chips piled high on the table.

1824: Lafayette Deck This deck was manufactured by Jazaniah Ford of Milton, Massachusetts, who is credited as the first known maker of playing cards in the United States. The deck was issued to honor the French hero Marquis de Lafayette upon his return to the United States in 1824. Before the age of 20, Lafayette had become a Major General in Washington's army during the American Revolution and won many battles, participating in the final defeat of General Cornwallis on Oct.19, 1781.

Exceptionally Beautiful 1855 Samuel Hart & Co. Illuminated Deck This is thought to be the only example of this deck known and it is not listed in any catalog or encyclopedia. Collectors refer to these decks as "illuminated" because of the gold that was used extensively on the court cards and surrounding each pip on every card. (The term is borrowed from the illuminated manuscripts of medieval Europe.) Although deeply influenced by European designs, these standard one-way court cards are considered to be among the most beautiful ever produced in America and were accompanied by a patriotic Ace of Spades that showed the stars and stripes along with the eagle. The deck was produced by the well known mid-nineteenth century card manufacturer Samuel Hart & Co. of Philadelphia and New York.

Extremely rare 1819 cards known as the "Seminole War Deck," although it actually commemorates the Creek War of 1813 to 1814. It was manufactured by J.Y. Humphreys of Philadelphia. The cards were hand colored on printed engravings, with hand stencilled pips. Spades are blue, hearts are red, diamonds are yellow and clubs are green. George Washington appears as the King of Hearts, Thomas Jefferson as King of Clubs, Andrew Jackson as King of Spades and John Quincy Adams as King of Diamonds. The Queens are Greek and Roman Goddesses, Athena/Spades, Venus/Hearts, Ceres/Clubs and Justice/ Diamonds. Jacks or Knaves are the Indian Tribal leaders: Gy-ant-wachia as Jack of Diamonds, Joseph Brant, an Iroquois, as Jack of Clubs, and Red Jacket as Jack of Hearts. The Jack of Spades is unidentified.

February 7, 1864: "Saladee's Patent" Deck An historic milestone manufactured by Samuel Hart & Co. of Philadelphia and New York. This was the first deck to use Saladee's Patent, that is to print indices with the numbers and suit signs in the corners of the cards. This simple idea revolutionized the card manufacturing industry. It had taken centuries for someone to think of this innovation and it took 15 more years until it became the standard design of card manufacturers.

1865: Army and Navy Playing Cards A rare Civil War deck that collectors often refer to as the Monitor and Merrimac Deck, was manufactured in New York by Andrew Dougherty & Co. Quite unusual suit signs were employed in this deck. In place of Spades and Clubs, were blue images of the Monitor and Merrimac. Drummer Boys and Zouave soldiers were substituted for Hearts and Diamonds. On the Ace of Monitors it reads, "To Commemorate the Greatest Event in Naval History, the Substitution of Iron for Wood." The Kings, Queens and Jacks are symbolic caricatures of the Civil War era. The original wrapper has the words "Army and Navy" set against a starry sky with a Zouave holding the flag pole of an unfurling stripes.

These two decks by Nelson are eagerly sought after by Civil War collectors as well as card collectors, since only a handful of each are known to exist today. Oddly enough, Robert E. Lee and Jefferson Davis are on the three of hearts and nine of spades respectively but this was not northern bias since Ulysses S. Grant was placed on the five of diamonds in the Union deck.

Opposite:
1863: Officers in the Army of the Union A Civil War deck printed by Mortimer Nelson of New York. On the face of each card is an engraved portrait of a Union General or Northern Statesman. Nelson used miniatures of the more traditional card images in the upper left hand corners, making it easier to observe each card as they were spread in the hand. Nelson advertised on his wrapper that this layout of the card was an improvement in the design of playing cards. Numerical corner indices on cards had not yet been developed. In 1876, card manufacturer, Andrew Dougherty, patented and used Nelson's idea in his "Triplicate" decks, using miniature cards in the upper left and lower right corners of each card.

Above:
1863: Officers in the Rebel Army Collectors refer to this deck as "The Confederate Generals" or "Southern Generals" deck but on the printed wrapper of the deck Nelson referred to it as "Officers in the Rebel Army." Surprisingly, it was produced in the north by Mortimer Nelson of New York, but the same wrapper also described the earlier companion deck as "Officers in the Army of the Union," printed that same year. Here too, engraved portraits of officers and high government officials are shown on the faces of the 52 cards, while the more traditional card faces are shown as miniatures in the upper left hand corner of each card.

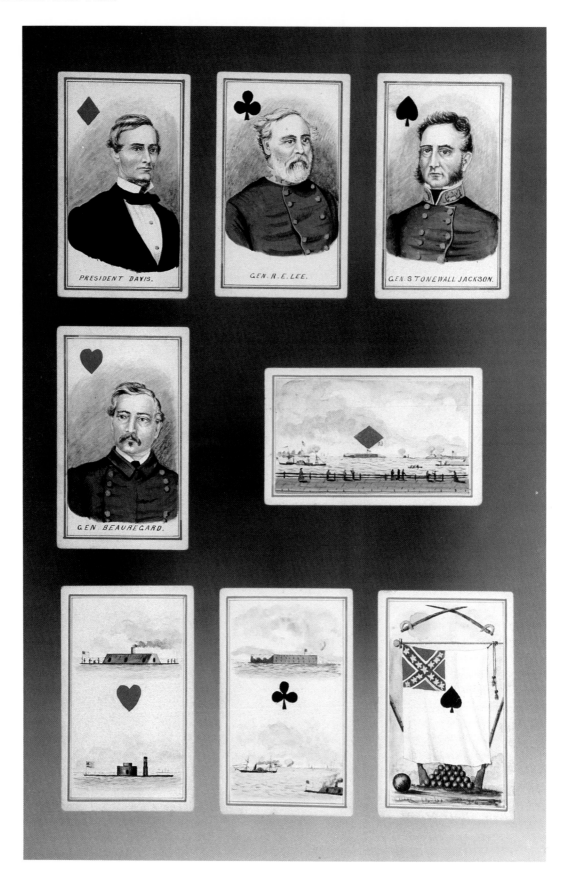

1864: Confederate Civil War Deck This unique hand-painted deck was created by Wm. Aiken Walker (1838-1921), a noted Southern American artist and Confederate cartographer. Each of the cards is painted with delicate brush strokes. The Kings portray Confederate President Jefferson Davis, General Robert E. Lee, General Stonewall Jackson and General P.G.T. Beauregard. The Ace of Spades shows the Confederate flag under crossed swords and hanging over a pyramid of cannon balls. The other Aces depict major battles of the Civil War, including the battle between the Monitor and Merrimac, the firing on Fort Sumter, and a Merrimac victory. Jacks and Queens include Confederate heroines, guards, buglers, and drummers. Walker also painted "Poker Game Aboard a Mississippi River Boat" in 1880 and many other fine paintings that are today sold in leading auction houses.

c. 1885: Whiskey Insert Cards Single cards of this deck were included as inserts with each pint or half pint of Deep Run Hunt Club Rye Whiskey made by E.A. Saunders' Sons' Co. of Richmond, Virginia. Realizing that those who collected these cards would probably acquire many duplicates, the company offered, on the back of each card, to send a full deck to anyone who sent 50 of these inserts to them. Similar pin-ups of the period were also used as insert cards in tobacco products such as Hard A Port, Kids, and Trumps, and by tobacco companies such as Lorillard, W. Duke & Sons, and Kinney.

Three Coca-Cola Decks Since 1909, numerous decks, each with different images, have been manufactured as advertising for the Coca-Cola company. In the center is an extremely rare 1915 deck showing a woman drinking Coca-Cola, attired in the Art Nouveau fashion of the day. On either side are two Coca-Cola decks from the period of World War II, each showing a woman wearing a military uniform.

The Lusitania and the United States Lines Decks The deck on the left was made for the two sister ships of the Cunard Lines, the famous Lusitania and the Mauritania. The luxury liner Lusitania was sunk by a German U-Boat on May 7th, 1915 off the coast of Ireland. 1198 passengers and crew died at sea, including 128 Americans. This was considered to be a pivotal event in the 1917 entry of the U.S. into the First World War against Germany. The United States Lines deck is from about the same period.

Opposite and above:
c. 1925-1935: Maxfield Parrish Decks These mysteriously beautiful and treasured images are from a series of ten decks produced for Edison Mazda Lampworks of General Electric Co. An extra card states, "The illustration on the back of these cards is from an original painting by Maxfield Parrish, the foremost living decorative American artist." These extra cards along with the Joker often added up to 54 or 55 cards per box, an important note for collectors. The titles of the ten decks are "Enchantment," "The Lamp Seller of Baghdad," "Venetian Lamplighter," "Spirit of Night," "Egypt," "The Waterfall," "Ecstasy," "Reveries," "Contentment" and "Night is Fled."

c. 1900-1910: Advertising Decks These turn of the century advertising decks were manufactured for various companies to help promote their products. The name of the product, along with a trademark image or logo appears on many or all sides of the box, on the backs of the cards, and on the Aces and Jokers. Tobacco and alcohol are the most likely products to be found on decks, but using playing cards to advertise and to promote good will was also practiced by department stores, automobile products, food products, and even telephone companies.

July, 1893: Calendar Sheet This 7.75" x 12" calendar was made by the United States Printing Co. in 1893. It was printed specifically for their "Main Eastern" branch office in Brooklyn. Lady Liberty, which became the permanent trademark of the United States Playing Card Co., is featured on this calendar page.

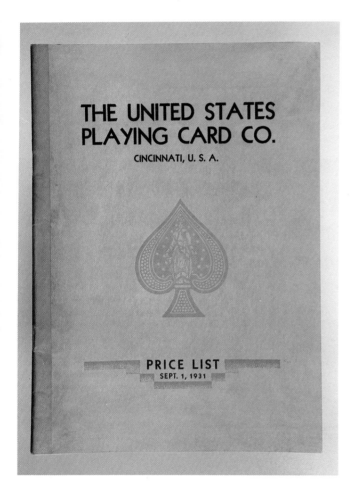

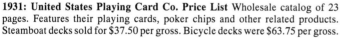

1931: United States Playing Card Co. Price List Wholesale catalog of 23 pages. Features their playing cards, poker chips and other related products. Steamboat decks sold for $37.50 per gross. Bicycle decks were $63.75 per gross.

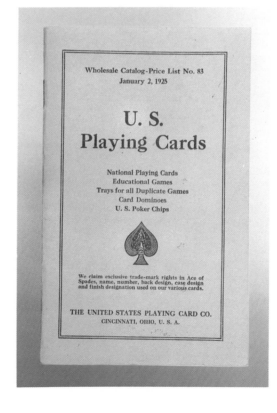

1925: United States Playing Card Co. Catalog This 51 page catalog contained the wholesale prices for those who bought decks of cards in large quantities. Steamboats were $40.35 per gross; rare Steamboat decks now cost between $200 and $300. Souvenir decks were $102 per gross; many Souvenir decks are now worth more than $102 per deck. A rare American Indian Souvenir deck available from this company in 1925, recently sold for $1,540. (See illustration of Souvenir Decks)

c. 1910: United States Playing Card Co. Postcard This postcard shows the building still occupied by the United States Playing Card Co. in Norwood, Ohio, a suburb of Cincinnati. The Russell & Morgan Co. went into business in 1881, and then became The Russell and Morgan Printing Co. in 1885. The name of the company was then changed to The United States Printing Co. in 1891, which in turn became the United States Playing Card Co. (USPC) in 1894, the name that is still used today.

c. 1885: Russell & Morgan Advertising Trade Card These 3" x 5.5" trade cards were distributed free as promotional material to their customers.

c. 1893: United States Printing Co. Advertisement This 8.5" x 11" ad, using the names Russell & Morgan Factories, as well as The United States Printing Co., appeared on the back cover of the program printed for the annual convention of lithographers, held in Cincinnati in 1893. The image of the king astride his bicycle was used as a Joker.

c. 1889: Bicycle Cards Sample Group of Jokers riveted together as promotional material for salespeople to show to owners of retail shops that sold United States Printing Co. (USPC) cards. This sample was from what was then the new Bicycle line by USPC. The image on the Jokers were men riding the then stylish high wheeled bicycles, marked with the term "Best Bower," an early term for the Joker. USPC Bicycle decks have now been made with over 80 different back designs and are a favorite of collectors.

c. 1891-1893: United States Printing Co. Trade Card Printed by United States Playing Card when it was known as The United States Printing Co. The King of Spades rides along on a bicycle to advertise the USPC line of Bicycle playing cards, pointing toward a billboard of their trademark Ace of Spades and wearing a back pack marked "Bicycle Cards." There are two cardboard disks on the back of the card, directly behind the bicycle wheels on the front. These rotate on a small rivet so that the numbers from one to ten can be seen inside the wheels on the front of the card, allowing card players to keep score.

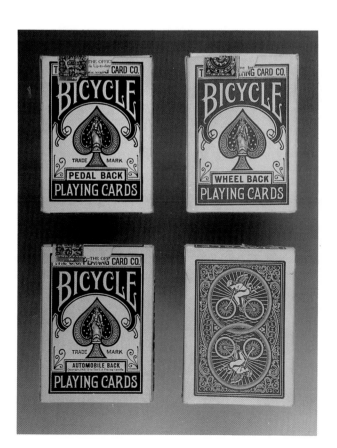

c. 1890-1910: USPC Bicycle Decks First manufactured in 1885, Bicycle decks were to become one of the most successful brand names of the United States Playing Card Co. There are over 80 different back designs on Bicycle cards, and some of those designs are still being manufactured today. They've been made in red, blue, green and brown; the last two are the most difficult to find since they were no longer made after 1927. The Joker shown is the first ever to be used with Bicycle decks.

1909: Jeffries Championship Deck Manufactured by W.P. Jeffries Co. of Los Angeles. Jim Jeffries, heavyweight boxing champion of the world in the early twentieth century, is pictured on the backs of the cards and on the Joker. On the faces of the cards are scenes from famous boxing matches and well known boxers of that time, such as John L. Sullivan, Gentleman Jim Corbett, Jack Johnson, Battling Nelson and many others.

1895: American Playing Card Co. Advertisement A 6.5" x 9.25" magazine advertisement promoting a brand from the American Playing Card Co. of Kalamazoo, Michigan. The brand name of "Golf" is echoed in the image of the young woman about to swing her golf club. Like the USPC, this company also used the patriotic symbols of eagles, flags and stars.

Opposite page
c. 1890-1900: Steamboat Decks Each company that manufactured playing cards had their own versions of a "Steamboat deck." These were the least expensive decks of each manufacturer's line. Various steamboats, some sidewheelers, so closely associated with gambling on the Mississippi riverboats, were used as illustrations on the boxes and often on the Aces and the Joker. These decks were made by Andrew Dougherty; New York Consolidated Card Co.; American Playing Card Co.; Standard Playing Card Co.; and Kalamazoo Playing Card Co.

1916: Movie Souvenir Deck The first known deck to use actors and actresses on each card was manufactured in 1882. It showed well known stars of the stage. Decks like this one, using photographs of famous actors and actresses of the movie screen followed several decades later. The idea of movie stars on decks is still popular today. The deck shown here may be the earliest of the Movie Souvenirs. The backs depict the chariot race from the original Ben Hur. What better choice could there have been than Charlie Chaplin for the Joker?

c. 1900 -1915: Souvenir Decks There are well over 100 known Souvenir decks that were made between 1890 and 1925. They were made for railroad lines, cities, states, national parks and expositions, along with those produced for commemorative events. Although many of the backs are quite beautiful, the most interesting aspect of Souvenirs is that each face contains a different photograph of a particular area, route or topic. Upper left: Washington, D.C.; upper right: Father Knickerbocker/New York City; lower left: Panama Canal Inaugural; lower right: The American Indian Souvenir Deck.

Opposite page:
1879: Tiffany Transformation The actual name of this deck, as noted on the box and on the Ace, is "Harlequin Playing Cards." It was manufactured for Tiffany & Co. of New York, London and Paris, the company famous for its jewelry and stained glass. The deck was designed by C.E. Carryl. This type of deck is known as a "transformation" because the pips on every card are transformed into separate pictures, which then form an overall design on each card. Transformation decks are often quite clever and witty in the way the suit signs are incorporated into the pictures. Perhaps after reading this book, you too will have been transformed - into a collector of gambling memorabilia and antique playing cards.

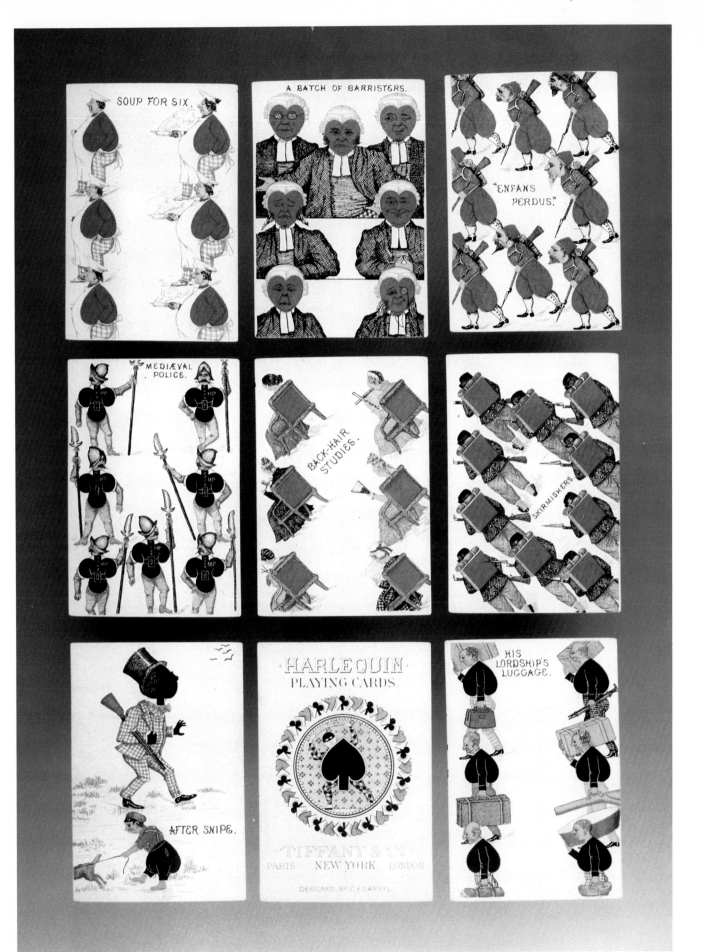

SUGGESTED READING LIST & BIBLIOGRAPHY FOR PLAYING CARDS

Each of the books listed here is worthy of keeping as part of your gambling and playing card collection and is also excellent for research. The most informative work about American playing cards is the comprehensive and pioneering six volume set of Gene Hochman's *The Encyclopedia of American Playing Cards.* This is a must for every collector. Soon to be released as a single volume. *(See Dawsons on Contact List)* Another extremely useful book is *A History of Playing Cards* by Catherine Perry Hargrave.

Benham, Sir Wm. Gurney. *Playing Cards; History of the Pack* and *Explanations of its Many Secrets.* London, Spring Books, 1957 (orig. pub.1931)

Cary, Melbert B. *War Cards.* New York, Press of the Woolly Whale, 1937.

Chatto, Wm. Andrew. *Facts and Speculations on the Origin and History of Playing Cards.* London, J.R. Smith, 1848.

Field, Albert "Cap". *Transformation Playing Cards.* Stamford, Connecticut, U.S. Games Systems Inc., 1987.

Hargrave, Catherine Perry. "The Playing Cards of New England". Boston, *The Bulletin of Old Time New England,* 1928.

_____. *A History of Playing Cards and a Bibliography of Cards and Gaming.* New York, Dover Publications Inc., 1966. (orig. pub. by Houghton Mifflin, 1930).

Hochman, Gene. *The Encyclopedia of American Playing Cards.* 6 Volumes, Livingston, New Jersey, Gene Hochman, 1976-1982.

Horr, Norton Townshend. *A Bibliography of Card-Games and of the History of Playing-Cards.* Cleveland, C. Orr, 1892.

Jessel, Frederic. *A Bibliography of Works in English on Playing Cards and Gaming.* London, Longmans Green, 1905.

Keller, Wm. B. *The Cary Collection of Playing Cards.* 4 Volumes, New Haven, Connecticut, Yale University Press, 1981.

Kurzrok, Lawrence. *United States Playing Cards Priced Catalogue.* New York, L. Kurzrok, 1965.

Mann, Sylvia. *Collecting Playing Cards.* New York, Crown Publishers, 1966.

Morley, Henry T. *Old and Curious Playing Cards.* London, Batsford, 1931.

Robinson, Joe Mrs. *Bicycle Brand Playing Cards.* 1955.

Singer, Samuel Weller. *Researches into the History of Playing Cards.* London, R. Triphook, 1816.

Smith, Patterson. *Bibliographies of Works on Playing Cards and Gaming.* Montclair, New Jersey, Patterson Smith, 1972.

Taylor, Edward Samuel. *The History of Playing Cards, with Anecdotes of Their Use in Conjuring, Fortunetelling, and Card-Sharping.* London, J.C. Hotten, 1865.

Tilley, Roger. *Playing Cards.* London, Weidenfeld & Nicholson, 1967.

Van Rensselaer, May (King). *The Devil's Picture Books; A History of Playing Cards.* London, T. Fisher Unwin, 1892.

_____. *Prophetical, Educational and Playing Cards.* London, Hurst & Blackett, 1912.

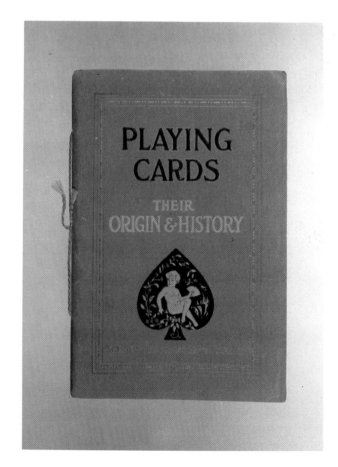

1916: Playing Cards, Their Origin and History by Stanley A. Cohen. Published by New York Consolidated Card Co. This 5" x 7" booklet of 31 pages is bound in a heavy weight parchment like paper with the cover printing and design embossed on the front cover.

SUGGESTED READING LIST & BIBLIOGRAPHY

Books are very helpful for doing research on gambling collectibles and they are also worthy collectibles themselves. A full bibliography of books on poker, chronologically arranged from 1836 to 1941, is at the end of Chapter One. Books written specifically about playing cards are at the end of Chapter Ten. There are also many books which have been used as illustrations throughout this book and information about them is in their caption material.

Arnold, Peter. *The Book of Gambling*. London, Hamlyn, 1974.
_____. *The Encyclopedia of Gambling*. Secaucus, New Jersey, Chartwell Books, 1977.
Asbury, Herbert. *Sucker's Progress*. New York, Dodd Mead, 1938.
_____. *The French Quarter: An Informal History of the New Orleans Underworld*. New York, Knopf, 1928.
_____. *The Barbary Coast: An Informal History of the San Francisco Underworld*. New York, Knopf, 1933.
Bailey, Robert. *Life and Adventures of Robert Bailey*. Richmond, Virginia, J. & G. Cochran, 1822.
Beecher, Henry Ward. *Gambling and Gamblers*. Philadelphia, Henry Altemus, 1896.
Bender, Eric J. *Tickets to Fortune*. New York, Modern Age Books, 1938.
Bohn, Henry George. *The Handbook of Games*. London, H.G. Bohn, 1850.
Brolaski, Harry. *Easy Money: All Gambling Tricks Exposed*. Cleveland, Searchlight Press, 1911.
Brunner, Robert. *Treasury of Gambling Stories*. Chicago, Ziff Davis, 1946.
Burdick, J.R. *The American Card Catalog*. East Stroudsburg, Pennsylvania, Kistler Printing Co., 1960.
Chafetz, Henry. *Play the Devil*. New York, C. N. Potter, 1960.
Collier, Wm. Ross. *The Reign of Soapy Smith*. New York, Doubleday Doran, 1935. (bio. of Jefferson Randolph Smith)
Comstock, Anthony. *Frauds Exposed*. New York, J.H. Brown, 1880.
Cox, Wm. R. *Luke Short and His Era*. New York, Doubleday, 1961.
Culin, Stewart. *Games of the North American Indians*. Washington, D.C., Government Printing Office, 1907.
Davis, Clyde Brion. *Something for Nothing*. Philadelphia, Lippincott, 1955.
DeArment, Robert K. *Knights of the Green Cloth*. Norman, OK., University of Oklahoma Press, 1990.
Devol, George H. *Forty Years a Gambler on the Mississippi*. Cincinnati, Devol & Haines, 1887.
Dodge, Harry. *Fifty Years at the Card Table*. Syracuse, NY, 1885.
Erdnase, S.W. (a reverse of E. S. Andrews) *Artifice, Ruse and Subterfuge at the Card Table*. Chicago, F.J. Drake, 1902.
Evans, Gerritt M. *How Gamblers Win; or the Advantage Player's Manual*. New York, G. M. Evans, 1865.
Ezell, John Samuel. *Fortune's Merry Wheel: The Lottery in America*. Cambridge, Harvard University Press, 1960.
Fabian, Ann. *Card Sharps, Dream Books, and Bucket Shops*. Ithaca, New York, Cornell University Press, 1990.
Figgis, E.L. *Focus on Gambling*. London, Barker Ltd., 1951.
Findlay, John M. *People of Chance*. New York, Oxford University Press, 1986.
Garcia, Frank. *Marked Cards and Loaded Dice*. New Jersey, Prentice-Hall, 1962.
Gardiner, Alexander. *Canfield; The True Story of the Greatest Gambler*. New York, Doubleday Doran, 1930.
Gibson, Walter B. *The Bunco Book*. Holyoke, Massachusetts, Sidney H. Radner, 1946.
Glasscock, C.B. *Lucky Baldwin: The Story of an Unconventional Success*. New York, A.L. Burt, 1935. (biography of Elias Jackson Baldwin who built and owned Santa Anita Racetrack)
Green, Jonathan Harrington. *An Exposure of the Arts and Miseries of Gambling*. Cincinnati, U.P. James, 1843.
_____. *Gambling Unmasked*. New York, Burgess, Stringer & Co. 1844.
_____. *The Gambler's Mirror*. Baltimore, Wm. Taylor, 1845.
_____. *The Secret Band of Brothers*. Philadelphia, G.B. Zeiber, 1847.
_____. *Gambling in its Infancy and Progress*. New York, Colby, 1849.
_____. *Twelve Days in the Tombs; or, A Sketch of the Last Eight Years of a Reformed Gambler's Life*. Baltimore, Wm. Taylor, 1850.
_____. *A Report on Gambling in New York*. New York, J.H. Green, 1851.
_____. *Gambling Exposed*. Philadelphia, T.B. Peterson, 1857.
_____. *The Reformed Gambler*. Philadelphia, T.B. Peterson, 1858.
_____. *The Gambler's Life*. Philadelphia, T.B. Peterson, 1858.
_____. *Gambler's Tricks With Cards, Exposed and Explained*. New York, Dick & Fitzgerald, 1859.
Guild, Leo. *The World's Greatest Gambling Systems*. Los Angeles, Sirkay Publishing, 1966
Hendricks, Wm. *History of Pool, Billiards and Snooker*. Roxana, Illinois, Wm. Hendricks, 1989
Hicks, Jim, ed. *The Gamblers*. Alexandria, Virginia, Time Life Books, 1978.
Hoyle, Edmond. *Hoyle's Games*. Philadelphia, Henry F. Anners, 1845.
Hugard, Jean. *Card Manipulations*. New York, Max Holden, 1935.
Hunter, H.E. *How 'Tis Done, or the Secret Out*. New Hampshire, Hunter & Co. 1864
Johnson, John Hugh. *The Open Book*. Kansas City, Missouri, 1926.
Katcher, Leo. *The Big Bankroll; the Life and Times of Arnold Rothstein*. New York, Harper, 1959.
Lenihan, Maurice. *If You Must Gamble*. New York, J.F. Wagner, 1946.

Lewis, Oscar. *Sagebrush Casinos*. New York, Doubleday & Co., 1953.

Long, Mason. *The Life of Mason Long, the Converted Gambler*. Chicago, Donnelley & Co., 1878.

Ludovici, L.J. *The Itch for Play*. London, Jarrolds, 1962.

MacDougall, Michael. *Danger in the Cards*. Chicago, Ziff Davis, 1943.

_____. *Gamblers Don't Gamble*. New York, Greystone Press, 1939.

Maskelyne, John Nevil. *Sharps and Flats*. London, Longmans, Green, 1894.

Mastroly, Frank. *Pittsburgh Phil: A Novel of a Legend*. New York, Duell Sloan & Pearce, 1960.

McQuaid, Clement. *Gambler's Digest*. Chicago, Follett, 1971.

Meyer, Joseph Ernest. *Protection: The Sealed Book*. Milwaukee, J.E.Meyer, 1911.

Olmstead, Charlotte. *Heads I Win, Tails You Lose*. New York, Macmillan, 1962

Ortiz, Darwin. *Gambling Scams*. New York, Dodd, Mead & Co., 1984.

Paher, Stanley W. ed. *Nevada: Towns and Tales*. Las Vegas, Nevada, Nevada Publications, 1982.

Parlett, David. *A History of Card Games*. New York, Oxford University Press, 1991.

Powell, Stephen. *A Gambling Bibliography*. Las Vegas, University of Las Vegas Press, 1972.

Quinn, John Philip. *Fools of Fortune*. Chicago, G.L. Howe & Co., 1890.

_____. *Gambling and Gambling Devices*. Canton, Ohio, J.P. Quinn Co., 1912.

_____. *Nineteenth Century Black Art or Gambling Exposed*. Chicago, J.P. Quinn Publishing, 1891.

Radner, Sidney H. *How to Spot Card Sharps and Their Methods*. New York, Key Publishing Co., 1957.

_____. *How to Play Poker and Win*. Baltimore, Ottenheimer Publishers, 1957

Rice, Cy. *Nick the Greek: King of the Gamblers*. New York, Funk & Wagnalls, 1969.

Robertson, Frank Chester. *Soapy Smith: King of the Frontier Con Men*. New York, Hastings House, 1961.

Romain, Harold James. *Gambling*. Chicago:, Craig Press, 1891

Scarne, John. *Scarne on Cards*. New York, Crown Publishers, 1949.

_____. *The Odds Against Me: An Autobiography*. New York, Simon & Schuster, 1966

_____. *The Complete Guide to Gambling*. New York, Simon & Schuster, 1961.

Seymour, Dale. *Antique Gambling Chips*. Palo Alto, CA., Past Pleasures, 1985.

_____. *Ivory Poker Chips*. Palo Alto, CA., Past Pleasures, 1987.

Smith, Matthew Hale. *Sunshine and Shadow in New York*. Hartford, CT., J.B. Burr, 1868.

Smith, Patterson. "The Literature of Gambling" in *A.B. Bookman's Weekly*, May 6, 1985

Trumble, Alfred. *Faro Exposed*. New York, Richard K. Fox, 1882.

"Trumps". *The American Hoyle*. New York, Dick & Fitzgerald, 1864.

Wallace, Frank R. *Poker: A Guaranteed Income for Life*. New York, Warner Books, 1978.

Walsh, Audley V. *A Treatise on Three Card Monte*

Warshow, Robert Irving. *Bet-A-Million Gates: The Story of a Plunger*. New York, Greenberg, 1932. (Bio. of John Warne Gates 1855-1911)

Wommack, Linda. *Colorado Gambling: A History of the Early Days*. Denver, 1991.

Wykes, Alan. *The Complete Illustrated Guide to Gambling*. New York, Doubleday, 1964.

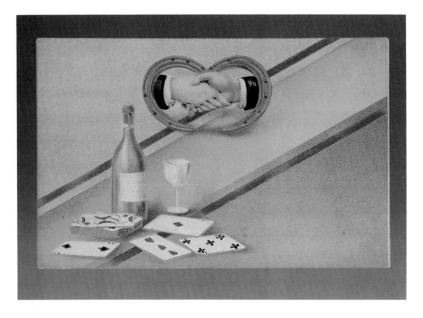

1908: Handshake Postcard Embossed. This warm and cordial message seems to say that friendship, fair play, good sportsmanship, and a bit of luck as suggested by the horseshoes, are a prerequisite for a good game of cards.

CONTACTS

The following people, organizations and periodicals are excellent sources of information about various aspects of gambling collectibles. Always include a self addressed, stamped envelope when requesting information.

LEONARD SCHNEIR (your author) I welcome any reader of this book to write to me. Let me know about any additions, suggestions, changes or corrections that you feel might be helpful for the next printing. I'd also be pleased to hear from you about your discoveries of gambling collectibles and about your collection. P.O. Box 266, Village Station, New York, NY 10014.

52 + JOKER An excellent and exciting organization with over 400 members devoted to collecting playing cards and gambling collectibles. This club has a very informative, well illustrated quarterly bulletin called "Clear the Decks". Annual conventions for lectures, auctions, trading, buying and selling. Contact: Rhonda Hawes, 204 Gorham Ave., Hamden, CT 06514.

GENE ARNOLD For theater lobby cards. 2234 South Blvd., Houston, TX 77098

ROGER BAKER For ivory chips, pharo, general. P.O. Box 620417, Woodside, CA 94062

PHIL BEGUHL For ivory chips, pharo. P.O. Box 6886, Santa Barbara, CA 93160

TOM BLUE For poker, pharo, books, cheating devices. 6637 Colbath, Van Nuys, CA 91405

PHIL BOLLHAGEN For playing cards. P.O. Box 20998, Greenfield, WI 53220

STEVE BOWLING For ivory chips. 1515 Centre Point Drive, Milpitas, CA 95035.

RICHARD BUESCHEL For slot machines. Author of the *Illustrated Price Guide for Slot Machines and Trade Stimulators*. 414 N. Prospect Manor Ave., Mount Prospect, IL 60056.

AL CALI For dice, chuck-a-luck, general. 19939 Charters Ave., Saratoga, CA 95070

CASINO CHIPS & GAMING TOKENS CLUB P.O. Box 63, Brick, NJ 08723

"THE CARD PLAYER" A monthly magazine. Excellent on contemporary gambling and casinos.1455 East Tropicana Ave. Suite 450, Las Vegas, NV 89119

KEN CHOPPING For ivory chips. 145 Cresta Drive, #2, San Rafael, CA 94903.

CLASSIC IMAGES An organization for Hollywood memorabilia. P.O. Box, 809, Muscatine, IA 52761.

KEN CRAIG For ivory chips. 3927-H Waring Rd., Oceanside, CA 92056

STEVE CROWLEY For pharo, general. c/o SCA Real Estate, 166 Kings H'way North, Westport, CT 06880.

TOM and JUDY DAWSON For playing cards, books, ephemera. If you are interested in the single volume of the "Encyclopedia of American Playing Cards," write to the Dawsons. One, Benlamond Drive, Toronto, Ontario, M4E 1Y6, Canada.

TOBY EDWARDS For playing cards. 207 E. 15th St., Apt. 6C, New York, NY 10003

ROBERT EISENSTADT For ivory & clay chips. P.O. Box 767, Brooklyn, NY 11202

DAVID GALT For games and playing cards. 302 W. 78th St., New York, NY 10024

GAMBLER"S BOOK CLUB Great selection of contemporary and out of print books on gambling. Catalog available. 630 South 11th St., Las Vegas, NV 89101

GAMING RESOURCE CENTER Excellent for research. James R. Dickinson Library, 4505 Maryland Parkway, The University of Nevada, Las Vegas, NV 89154. Director: Susan Jarvis

GEORGE GIUMARRA For pharo, cheating devices, general. P.O. Box 176, Edison, CA 93220

BERNIE GOLD For slot machines, coin operated machines. P.O. Box 1306, Great Neck, NY 11023

BOB HARRISON For playing cards. 582 Woodlawn, Glencoe, IL 60022

RAY HARTZ For playing cards. Currently president of 52 + Joker. P.O. Box 1002, Westerville, OH 43081

STEVE HOWARD For ivory chips, pharo, general. 101 First St., Suite 404, Los Altos, CA 94022

INTERCOL For world-wide antique and modern playing cards. Catalog available. 43 Templars Crescent, London N3 3QR England

LARRY LUBLINER For books, gambling watches, advertising. Annual catalog for mail/phone auctions of gambling collectibles. Also carries 6 vol. set of Hochman *Encyclopedia on American Playing Cards*. P.O. Box 1501, Highland Park, IL 60035.

ALLAN MYERS For ivory & casino chips. Box 17002, Louisville, KY 40217

STEVE PASSALACQUA For all chips. 1035 La Quinta Court, Napa, CA 94559

"PAST TIMES" A newsletter about antique advertising. P.O. Box 1121, Morton Grove, IL 60053

SIDNEY RADNER For cheating devices, books, general. 1050 North Hampton St., Holyoke, MA 01040.

ROBERT ROSENBERGER For books, pharo, poker, cheating devices. 6592 Madeira Hills Drive, Cincinnati, OH 45243

DALE SEYMOUR For ivory chips. c/o Past Pleasures, Author of *Antique Gambling Chips* and *A Collector's Guide to Ivory Poker Chips*. P.O. Box 50863, Palo Alto, CA 94303.

ROD STARLING For playing cards. 4515 Bedford Ave., Brooklyn, NY 11235

"TIN TYPE" A newsletter about antique advertising. P.O. Box 440101, Aurora, CO 80044

RUSSELL UMBRACO For pharo, cheating devices, advertising. P.O. Box 5331, Richmond, CA 94805.

BYRON WALKER For books on gambling and magic. P.O. Box 3186, San Leandro, CA 94578

RON WOHL For gambling prints, cheating devices, books. P.O. Box 385, Cedar Knolls, NJ 07927

PRICE GUIDE

The prices listed here are for items in excellent to near mint condition. They reflect previous sales or the value of the item decided upon between knowledgeable collectors or at an auction. By far, the most important factor is that mint and near mint items are often worth dramatically more than those in less perfect condition. The following is a short list of the major factors that affect pricing: condition, supply, demand, state of the economy, whims of collectors, popularity of items at any particular time, and the financial conditions, patience and knowledge of buyers and sellers. All of these factors make it impossible to present an accurate price list, but these prices are offered as a guide.

The left hand number indicates the page.

The following abbreviations are used:
   T=top; B=bottom; L=left;
   R=right; M=middle.

Page	Pos	Price
1		5000-7500
2	T	20-30
4		20-30
5		35-45 ea.
6		20-30
7		6000-8000
8		5-10
9	L	250-350
9	R	600-800
9	M	250-350
10	L	20-30
10	R	20-30
10	M	25-35
10	B	200-300
11		100-200
12		150-200
13		200-300
14	T	50-75
14	B	125-175
15	T	400-600
15	B	600-800
16		250-350 ea.
17		250-350 ea.
18	LT	600-800
18	RT	250-350
18	LB	200-300
18	RB	750-1000
19	T	750-1000 ea.
19	M	300-400
19	B	300-400
20	LT	100-150
20	RT	300-400
20	LB	150-250
20	RB	150-250
21		1500-2500
22	LT	200-300
22	RT	100-150
22	LM	150-250
22	RM	150-200
22	B	500-750
23	LT	100-150
23	RT	100-150
23	M	100-150
23	LB	15-25 ea.
23	RB	25-50
24	T	1000-1500
24	B	100-150
25		25-35 ea.
26		25-35 ea.
26	RB	10-20
27	T	25-35
28		150-250
30		35-45 ea
31		10-20
32		25-35 ea.
33		25-35 ea.
34		25-35 ea.
35		35-45 ea.
35	RB	15-25
36		15-25 ea.
36	B	30-40
37	RT	15-25
37	LT	15-25
37	RB	30-40
37	LB	30-40
38	T	5-10 ea.
38	LM	15-25
38	RM	15-25
38	B	15-25
39	LT	40-50
39	RT	30-40
39	LM	30-40
39	LB	20-30
39	RB	35-45
40	T	40-50
40	M	30-40
40	B	20-30
41	LT	30-40
41	RM	30-40
41	LM	20-30
41	LB	20-30
41	RB	25-35
42		35-45 ea.
43	T	20-30
43	M	30-40
43	B	15-25
44	T	3000-5000
44	B	2000-3000
45		500-750
46	T	75-125
46	R	50-75; 15-25
46	B	750-1000
47	T	750-1000
47	R	10-20 ea.
47	LB	15-25 ea.
47	RB	150-250
48	LT	250-350
48	RT	25-50
48	M	10-20
48	B	50-100; 25-50
49	T	10-20 ea.
49	B	25-35
50	LT	200-300
50	RT	150-250
50	M	100-150
50	LB	50-75
50	RB	50-75
51		20-30 ea.
52		25-35 ea.
53		25-35
54	T	10-20
54	M	20-30
54	B	15-25
55		15-25 ea.
56		15-25 ea.
57		15-25 ea.
58		15-25 ea.
59		20-30 ea.
60		15-25 ea.
61		15-25 ea.
62		150-250
63		15-25
64		75-125 ea.
65		75-125 ea.
66	L	500-750
66	R	150-250
67	RT	100-150
67	LT	50-100
67	LB	100-150
67	RB	150-250
68	T	75-125
68	M	75-125
68	B	150-250
69	T	75-125
69	B	50-75
70	T	125-175
70	B	75-125
71		1500-2500
72		125-175
73		200-300
75		150-200
76		100-150
77		125-175
78		150-250
79		250-350
80		150-250
81	L	150-250
81	R	1500-2000
82		150-200 ea.
83	L	100-150
83	R	10-20
83	B	10-20
84		40-60 ea.
85		200-300
88		1500-2500
89		2000-3000
90		1250-1750
91		1500-2000
92	T	600-800
92	RB	150-250
93	LT	400-600
93	RT	1000-1500
93	LM	300-500
93	LB	1000-1500
93	RB	1500-2500
94	T	1000-1500
94	B	750-1250
95		15-25 ea.
96		25-35 ea.
97		25-45 ea.
99		800-1200
100	T	30,000-50,000
100	M	750-1000
100	B	10,000-15,000
101	T	5000-7500
103	LT	750-1250
103	B	500-750
107		800-1200
108	T	800-1200
108	M	1500-2500
109	T	1500-2000
109	B	600-800
110	LT	300-500
110	RT	800-1200
110	LB	500-750
110	RB	500-750
111	T	500-750
111	M	750-1000
111	B	600-800
112		10,000-15,000
114		15-25 ea.
115		2000-3000
116	LT	25-50
116	RT	25-50
116	B	1500-2500
117	LT	1000-1500
117	M	400-600
117	RT	1000-1500
117	LB	1000-1500
117	RB	400-600
118	LT	750-1000
118		400-600 ea.
119	T	25-35
119	B	125-175
120	T	500-750
120	B	800-1200 ea.
121		20-30 ea.
122	T	150-250 ea.
122	B	20-30 ea.
123	T	25-50
123	M	50-75
123	B	10-20
124		75-125 ea.
125		25-50
126	T	50-75
126	M	25-50
126	B	15-25
127		15-25 ea.
128		15-25 ea.
129		15-25 ea.
130		15-25 ea.
131		150-250
132		50-75
133		20-30
134		3000-5000
135		2000-3000
136		15,000-20,000
138		1000-1500
139		2500-3500
140		2500-3500
141		2500-3500
142		15,000-25,000
144		2500-3500
145	T	100-150; 2500-3500; 100-150
145	B	750-1000; 200-300
146		250-350 ea.
148		250-500 ea.
149	T	150-250
149	M	50-75
149	B	50-75
150		15-25 ea.
151	LT	75-125
151	RT	25-35
151	B	100-500
152		250-750
153	T	600-800
153	B	10-20
154	T	150-250
154	B	100-400
155		1250-1750
156		50-75
158		15-25